UNDERSTANDING

DONALD BARTHELME

Understanding Contemporary
American Literature

Matthew J. Bruccoli, *Editor*

UNDERSTANDING
Donald
BARTHELME

by STANLEY TRACHTENBERG

UNIVERSITY OF SOUTH CAROLINA PRESS

Grateful acknowledgment is made for permission to reprint passages from the following works by Donald Barthelme:

Snow White, copyright © 1987 Donald Barthelme, reprinted with permission of Atheneum Publishers, an imprint of Macmillan Publishing Company.
Great Days, copyright © 1970, 1976, 1977, 1978, 1979 by Donald Barthelme, reprinted by permission of Farrar, Straus and Giroux, Inc.
Paradise, copyright © 1986 by Donald Barthelme, reprinted by permission of the Putnam Publishing Group.
The Dead Father, *City Life*, *Sadness*, and *Unspeakable Practices, Unnatural Acts*, copyright by Donald Barthelme, reprinted with permission of the Estate of Donald Barthelme.

Published in Columbia, South Carolina, by the
University of South Carolina Press

Manufactured in the United States of America

Library of Congress Cataloging-in-Publication Data

Trachtenberg, Stanley.
    Understanding Donald Barthelme / by Stanley Trachtenberg.
        p. cm. — (Understanding contemporary American literature)
    Includes bibliographical references and index.
    ISBN 0-87249-711-9
    1. Barthelme, Donald—Criticism and interpretation.   I. Title.
II. Series.
PS3552.A76Z87   1990
813'.54—dc20   90-12687

For Rena and Sol Kunis

CONTENTS

EDITOR'S PREFACE

Understanding Contemporary American Literature has been planned as a series of guides or companions for students as well as good nonacademic readers. The editor and publisher perceive a need for these volumes because much of the influential contemporary literature makes special demands. Uninitiated readers encounter difficulty in approaching works that depart from the traditional forms and techniques of prose and poetry. Literature relies on conventions, but the conventions keep evolving; new writers form their own conventions—which in time may become familiar. Put simply, *UCAL* provides instruction in how to read certain contemporary writers—identifying and explicating their material, themes, use of language, point of view, structures, symbolism, and responses to experience.

The word *understanding* in the series title was deliberately chosen. Many willing readers lack an adequate understanding of how contemporary literature works; that is, what the author is attempting to express and the means by which it is conveyed. Although the criticism and analysis in the series have been aimed at a level of general accessibility, these introductory volumes are meant to be applied in conjunction with the works they cover. Thus they do not provide a substitute for the works and authors they introduce, but rather prepare the reader for more profitable literary experiences.

M. J. B.

UNDERSTANDING
DONALD BARTHELME

CHAPTER ONE

An Adequate Response to the World

Career

The oldest of five children, Donald Barthelme was born April 7, 1931, in Philadelphia, where both parents had attended the University of Pennsylvania. His father, a noted architect, who was trained in the beaux arts tradition of meticulous draftsmanship, soon moved the family to Houston, where, much in advance of his time, he developed an interest in the modernism of Le Corbusier, Mies van der Rohe, and Alvar Aalto, who, Barthelme noted, were interested not only in aesthetics but in the possibility of improving human existence.[1] Their influence, which Barthelme acknowledges as visually and spiritually important to him, was felt most immediately in the home his father designed for the family. Barthelme describes it as somewhat weird, although beautiful and similar to Mies van der Rohe's Tugendhat House.

Though he contends there is very little autobiography in his work, Barthelme acknowledges the influence of his mother, who he describes as a "wicked wit." In addition to the relative sophistication of his home environment, Barthelme recalls growing up surrounded by country music, such as that of Bob Wills and the Texas Playboys, and being strongly moved by the jazz of such greats as Erskine Hawkins, the pianist Peck Kelly, Lionel Hampton, and Louis Armstrong, whose playing gave him a sense of "making a statement, placing emphases within a statement or introducing variations."[2] Barthelme's association with contemporary painters and his interest in contemporary painting and literature did not so much serve to provide models for his own writing as a sense of the possibilities open to a writer. His story "Captain Blood," for example, is not a parody, he insisted, but an attempt to present or recall the essence of the subject which prompted it, in this case, the writer Raphael Sabatini.[3]

Barthelme was educated in Texas, where he attended the University of Houston as a journalism major and worked for the *Houston Post*. Drafted in 1953, he was stationed in Korea, returning to Houston two years later, where he worked in the public relations department of the university and studied philosphy with Maurice Natanson. He also founded the University of Houston *Forum*, a literary journal, whose contributors included Walker Percy, William H. Gass, Leslie Fiedler, Leonard Baskin, and Henri Cartier-Bresson. In 1959, Barthelme, who was on the board of trustees, became director of Houston's Contemporary Arts Museum, a post which brought him into contact with the art critic Harold Rosenberg and led to an invitation for Barthelme to edit the arts and literature magazine *Location*, which Rosenberg was planning in New York along with Thomas Hess. The journal lasted only two issues and Barthelme returned to Houston, where he taught part of the year at the University of Houston while maintaining his home in the Greenwich Village area of New York City, whose stimulating if messy vitality he compared to the collages of the artist Kurt Schwitters.

In 1974–75, Barthelme served as a Distinguished Visiting Professor of English at the City College of the City University of New York. Seen by some as a worthy successor to Franz Kafka, whose work stands as a touchstone for narrative art of the last two decades, Barthelme has been placed in the front rank of postmodernist writers along with John Barth, John Hawkes, Thomas Pynchon, and Italo Calvino. In 1971, he won the National Book Award in the juvenile literary category for his book *The Slightly Irregular Fire Engine; or the Hithering Thithering Djinn*, which he also illustrated.

Donald Barthelme died of cancer in Houston on July 23, 1989. He was 58 years old. Barthelme fondly recalled childhood visits with his grandfather, a rancher and lumber dealer in Galveston, whose home on the Guadalupe River not far from San Antonio the writer described as "a wonderful place to ride and hunt, talk to catfish and try to make the windmill run backward."[4] With the appropriate changes, those encounters with the windmill at times appear to reflect the way in which much of his fiction is written.

Overview

Defending formal innovation in the work of a group of American writers of the sixties, Donald Barthelme found a sustaining principle in popular fiction—he pointed to the impact of the Rover Boys, Tom Swift, *The Motion Picture Boys' First Venture*—which relied on the sentimental, the ingenuous, the trivial for much of its effect. Such fiction, Barthelme contended:

dispenses with characters, action, plot, and fact, dispenses with them by permitting them to proliferate all over the landscape and by resolutely short-circuiting the expected order of things. There is continual handling and mishandling of sentimental cliches. . . . There is pure linguistic play with abrupt changes of mood and intentionality. . . . Things lump themselves together in apparently random fashion.[5]

Barthelme traces this strategy to the example of James Joyce and Gertude Stein, later to that of Samuel Beckett, whose comedy caused fiction to alter its place in the world; that is to say, caused the displacement of character, social fact, and plot by language. After these writers, fiction had to be regarded less as a reflection of the

AN ADEQUATE RESPONSE TO THE WORLD

existing world or even as a commentary on it than as an object in itself, an object, as Barthelme says, "which is then encountered in the same way as other objects in the world . . . something that is there, like a rock or a refrigerator."[6] In Barthelme's story, "Sentence," for example, the disappearance of the architect Mies van der Rohe into one of his more famous houses reminds the reader that "the sentence itself is a man-made object," which though in many ways like other constructions, is "to be treasured for its weakness, as opposed to the strength of stones."[7]

One aspect of that weakness would seem to be the fluid quality that allows fictive constructions to resist interpretation and so preserve their magical properties.[8] Words, Barthelme maintains, are not inert, but furiously busy. In that movement, fiction does not so much provide a compensatory or even distractive balance to the inadequacy of experience—sexual, marital, filial, even, it turns out, linguistic. Rather it immerses the reader directly in that experience. Accordingly readers have difficulty identifying in his work a narrative voice outside the action which connects it to a system of values or beliefs, even to a designated set of attitudes or feelings that would allow them to interpret a story or indicate how they are expected to react to it. For Barthelme it is the loss of reference to the world that emerges as perhaps the most troubling aspect of contemporary culture, a loss that he traces in large measure to the deterioration of language. Meanings are not so much discovered or even created through the language of his fiction. In the absence of such meanings—or more accurately in the attempt to discourage those that have conventionally attached themselves to language and so obscured its graphic power—Barthelme's stories convey the agility of words to draw upon their prior history and so, as Barthelme has put it, allow the world to smuggle itself into the work.

Barthelme's prescription for fiction, of course, can't be read literally. What his fiction draws upon most of all, perhaps, is the ability of language to look both ways—transparently toward the world and self, apparently toward the mediating function of other words upon each other. Additionally Barthelme frustrates conventional structural expectations by blurring or exchanging the positions held by the antagonists in a conflict, indefinitely postponing a climax, or even by substituting the movement of linguistic elements for that of the characters whose lives they describe. This strategy of semantic or syntactic displacement through which words are paired in unlikely combinations allows Barthelme to create fantastic situations which the participants regard, if not precisely as ordinary, then at least as nothing much to be alarmed about. The much-remarked-upon inaccessibility of Barthelme's fiction can be seen, then, as response, not to the difficulties presented by the world, but to the formal literary conventions which distract from it. In short, in this fiction there is no inward look at what is going on.

AN ADEQUATE RESPONSE TO THE WORLD

What emerges as a defining element of Barthelme's fiction, then, is a tendency which, like abstract painting, is significant for what it subtracts from conventional form. There is no linear development (beginning, middle, end) either within his stories or from one collection to the next. Motivation remains unclear or, at best, arbitrary. Within the narrative there is no focus which allows for development, no clear indication of an agent whose purpose generates the action, an antagonist or natural force who opposes this purpose, a deepening or complication of the circumstances, and a final confrontation followed by a resolution which points up or explains the significance of what has happened. There is, in short, no distinction between background and foreground to identify a center of interest and not even an expressive or tonal variation which might itself serve to comment on events and so give them coherence.

To understand Barthelme's renewal of language it becomes necessary to look, not to the material world for some presumptive source of meaning but to the context established by words themselves. His response to the confusion and the consequent sense of incongruity experienced in even the most innocuous encounter is to incorporate in a single story alternate orders of experience—sometimes in disconnected conversations or objects or expressions that seem to come from different historical periods, sometimes in a mixture of various literary genres such as the western, the historical romance, the utopian fiction—without establishing a point of reference from which they can be seen to make sense. Symmetrical in shape, recurrent in structure, these fictions neutralize time and space, disolving not only the nature of reality but the esthetic process by which it is conventionally made to yield some sort of meaning. What remains is something outside the narrator's subjective perception, something, in fact, that establishes its reality precisely because it does not take its shape from the person or voice through which it is viewed. In the play of these two contrasting impulses— the play of language and the attractive pull of the world—lies much of the tension in the stories.

Though straining, at least in part, toward the world, whose modalities it faithfully records often in recognizable speech patterns or in objects drawn from popular culture, Barthelme's fictions are far from realistic. Realism, even qualified by the "magic" qualities which identify its postmodern forms, advances an illusion of reality dependent upon consistency, unified perspective, predictability, dimension, and scale. Barthelme's fiction, in contrast, offers only a minimal organization of experience, distilling and flattening its images so that in place of a textured world everything becomes a prop. Above all, however, this literalism is not realist because the fate of the characters is not determined by what has happened to them or by any force they can exert against it.

At the same time, Barthelme's fiction is distinct from those metafictional writers who took their cue

AN ADEQUATE RESPONSE TO THE WORLD

from Jorge Luis Borges or Vladimir Nabokov and abandoned meaning to celebrate the act of writing in mirrored inventions that lead neither toward nor away from reality but became suspended or entrapped in infinite regressions between it and the self. Barthelme directs the reader away from the tendency to reduce everything to fiction, even the self, perhaps the self most of all. Despite the questionnaire that he introduced in the middle of *Snow White* and the occasional revelation that the characters of a story serve as surrogates for yet another fictional presence, Barthelme has maintained that he has "no great enthusiasm for fiction-about-fiction."[9] Like the art of the period which rejected self-expression—abstract or otherwise—such writing could no longer identify an assured sense of self to express. It addressed the fictionality of fiction and in this way reminded the reader of the world of which it was a part. In contrast to the attempt to separate things from signs, which has often mistakenly been seen in his work, Barthelme does not displace meaning from the world to the text. Where such a deconstructive strategy challenges or at least exposes institutionalized signs of power, Barthelme attempts to restore the solidity of the world dissolved by the Impressionists; that is to say, attempts to reclaim space. Where the slogan of modernism was make it new, Barthelme resolves to make it *look* like new. Writing in a lyrical mode, he reduces the presence of the artist to the same plane as that of his art.

Barthelme's concern for the concrete object can be

seen in the catalogs or lists that frequently arrest the flow of narrative. These catalogs do not serve merely as displays of virtuosity. Originating in the formulaic imperatives of an oral tradition, the catalog conventionally testified to the vastness of events or the genealogical or geographic histories or rules of conduct that informed biblical and homeric texts. Subsequently they allowed the expression of Rabelaisian verve and exhuberance that parodied such epic displays. More recently, the catalog has emerged in the patter songs of Gilbert and Sullivan, of Cole Porter, and in the comic lists by which such writers as F. Scott Fitzgerald, Thomas Wolfe, or Sinclair Lewis both parodied and celebrated the acquisitive impulse of modern society or by which John Barth demonstrates—really exhausts—verbal possibilities.

In Barthelme's fiction, the catalog neither nostalgically commemorates the objects or events that evoke a historical moment nor plays with the seemingly infinite elaborations of reality that present themselves to the literary imagination. Its intent, in fact, is not so much illustration or expansion at all as it is the celebration of reality through repetition. Unlike those found in Whitman, Barthelme's catalogs do not name things which, almost mystically, exist by virtue of an incantatory act that demonstrates a unity in time and space. That unity does inform Barthelme's ennumeration, but it does not call things into being or magically summon

AN ADEQUATE RESPONSE TO THE WORLD

their presence; it reminds the reader of their unique and unknowable nature.

As an interruption of the narrative, the catalog or list seems merely another aspect of the difficulty in gaining access to Barthelme's fiction. The difficulty the reader experiences is one of orientation to events that seem to resemble those of the world but are governed by laws that have little relation to it, a world of antimatter. Often lists which are themselves taken from other listings—television programs, for example, or movie titles—the catalogs are not meant to establish unsuspected connections or suggest concealed meanings or emotions; on the contrary they are intended to document the ordinary and thus underscore its value. Such documentation is suggested in the concern for brand-name accuracy that informs Barthelme's often fantastic plots and invented facts. Barthelme has provided a clue to the importance of this specificity in a movie review he did for *The New Yorker* during a brief period when the regular reviewer was on vacation. Complaining of the anachronisms he found in a film set during the Second World War, Barthelme quoted with evident approval the architect Mies van der Rohe's famous dictum that God is in the details.[10]

More striking if elusive, illustrations of this strategy are the negative lists such as the animals who fail to arrive in "Views of My Father Weeping" or the unsuccessful though fully equipped knights in "The Glass Mountain," stories which appeared in *City Life*. Even more comprehensive is the list in "Nothing: A Preliminary Account" (*Guilty Pleasures*) which unsuccessfully attempts to embody nothingness. "If what exists is in each case the totality of the series of appearances which manifests it," Barthelme realizes, "then nothing must be characterized in terms of its non-appearances, no-shows, incorrigible tardiness."[11] Such lists have been identified by R. E. Johnson as part of a dialectic of retraction which locates, if at all, the beginnings and endings of Barthelme's fiction only outside its fictive boundaries.[12] For Johnson, the resulting obscurity is a function of the demand each of the stories makes to be viewed not only independently but also in the context of Barthelme's other stories, so that while the reality is predominantly linguistic in structure, it is continually being dissolved by the action of the story interrogating its own syntax. If, as Johnson further suggests, this resistance to formal structure means that the subject of the stories is displaced to the action by which it is perceived or to the failure of such perception, the movement of the fiction surely reflects a negative relation to imaginative forms at least as much as to the attempt the world makes to realize itself through them. Lists, then, even of nothing, provide the basis in language—at once suggestively dreamlike and reductively literal—for a continuing and continually urgent affirmation. These reductive tendencies were made available to modern

AN ADEQUATE RESPONSE TO THE WORLD

American art, and through it to Barthelme's own fiction, by a group of painters whose resistance to the dominant influences of the forties and fifties Barthelme has described as a "laboratory for everybody."[13] Among them he named Barnett Newman, whose work he saw "proceeding by subtraction"; Frank Stella, "rushing in the other direction"; and, most prominently, Ad Reinhardt, whose reduction of the image into monochromatic fields erased the revelations of modernism, clearing the way for a new syntax of visual forms that began with the surface of the canvas.[14] In contrast to the planes and angles by which cubism implied the tactility of space or the subsequent gesture by which abstract expressionism attempted to leave a record of the creative act in the application of paint to the canvas, Reinhardt took the timeless, formulaic schemes of Asian art as a model. Serious art, he proclaimed, needed to be symmetrical, preformed, routine, vacant rather than spontaneous, accidental, momentary, irrational. What was needed was a return to classical figural sculpture which, Reinhardt concluded, "has never lost its eloquence because it never says anything."[15]

In the visual terms which parallel and so illuminate Barthelme's fiction, this reductive strategy becomes particularly evident in the serial investigations of motif by artists such as Reinhardt, Newman, Albers, Louis, Noland, Stella, or Sol LeWitt, to name a few. These do not reveal a self-conscious preoccupation with formal issues but insist instead on a single repetitive, even decorative use of traditional elements. Emblematic or heraldic rather than symbolic, finite rather than ongoing, discrete rather than hierarchic, regulated or programmatic rather than improvised or spontaneous, still-photographic rather than cinematic, this reworking of an idea confines itself to a narrowly restricted scale of value differences and intensities. Alternatives do not cancel each other out but are contained or reinforced or suspended in necessarily humorous contradictions leaving tensions implicit or suggested rather than resolved through confrontation.

Though Barthelme has claimed to find conceptual art "a bit sterile," his fiction surprisingly reveals some striking parallels with the architectonic geometries of Sol LeWitt, whose system-derived art, like that of Barthelme's similar reaction against modernism, begins with the idea that drives it rather than arriving at that idea through the agency of technique.[16] "Since no form is intrinsically superior to another," LeWitt has insisted, "the artist may use any form, from an expression of words (written or spoken) to physical reality, equally."[17] All aspects, then, are reduced to a symmetry or sameness that denies unique compositional order and, even while establishing scale, tells us little about significance. Ultimately this reductive impulse emerged in an attempt to dematerialize, or at least deemphasize, the object in order to fuse the opposing ideas of structural order and random or aleatory movement, and extended even to LeWitt's willingness to have a work

AN ADEQUATE RESPONSE TO THE WORLD

executed by draftsmen rather than complete it in his own hand. This anonymity informs both the plan and execution which, along with the individual lines, LeWitt has claimed are all of equal importance.

What LeWitt attempts in form, however, Barthelme confines to content, and, in fact, LeWitt's disdain for formal invention and willingness to adopt an imitative style led to a controversy parodied in Barthelme's "Letters to the Editore" (*Guilty Pleasures*) in which an artist named LeDuff is accused of copying the work of European innovators. Despite Barthelme's suspicion of conceptualism, syntax itself becomes content. The minimal organization of material contrasts with the traditional relational structure through which meaning emerged by means of the balance or tension of individual elements. Barthelme's convoluted wordplay and seemingly taxidermic distancing frequently emerge in two-dimensional images that resemble the succession of frames in a cartoon strip. Characteristically the images derive from the permutations or progressions of a set of terms or conditions that are fundamentally repetitive and so allow for predictability without establishing causality. For Barthelme, as for the contemporary art whose influence his work reveals, form becomes not only separable from content but almost irrelevant to it, opacity not a consequence but an element of technique.

This austere style has often been seen as a reaction to the complex ironies of modernism, which attempted to reconcile the split between the expressive, the anarchic, the extreme, the subjective on the one hand and the impersonal, the traditional, the formal, the objective on the other. The protest of modernism led inescapably to a marginal posture or, more starkly, to a nihilistic one. It emerged through the central intelligence of Henry James or the oblique presentation and multiple points of view adopted by Joseph Conrad. In either case, from the immediacy of a world in which things existed, it looked, in James Joyce's now canonical description of the role of the artist, to a transcendent authority above or beyond or behind or within art where that world can be imagined. In a well-known and particularly apposite essay, Joseph Frank identified a change in the relation of the inward self to the outer world which reflected the modernist loss of belief in the ability to control natural forces and the consequent reduction of the world to linear or geometric forms.[18] Modernism sought to escape to the refuge of art where it could bring order to the chaotic or fragmented nature of events by perceiving them as a simultaneous occurrence. Frank designated the result spatial form. To arrive at that form, structure first had to be made disjunctive, typically through a loosening of metrical pattern and the inclusion of fragments of popular material normally excluded from serious art. The result, he saw, was cinematic in nature—a temporary suspension of the individual references of words that drew upon Mallarme's "ambition to create a language of 'absence' rather than of presence—a language in which words

AN ADEQUATE RESPONSE TO THE WORLD

negated their objects instead of designating them" (Frank 13).

In contrast to the modernists Frank discusses, Barthelme does not substitute for an unsatisfactory external world the more hospitable, interior one of art, hospitable because coherent. His words, even when they refer to the absence of things, are grounded in concrete experience. Barthelme does, however, employ a parallel interruption of sequence that denies, as in myth, the distinction between past and present. Such fiction distances itself from the world it represents through the cross cutting of plots, the sudden introduction of illustrative stories that have little connection to the main narrative, the blurring of interior levels of fiction and reality, or by interrogating the framing conditions of narrative. Events are not episodic but pictorial. At the same time, there is little sense of duration. Change is not simply *perceived* as an alteration of surface; it *occurs* only as such an alteration.

Barthelme's experimental treatment of syntactic logic frequently draws upon popular media such as movies, which, he explained, "provide a whole set of stock situations, emotions, responses that can be played against. They inflect contemporary language."[19] These elements are not combined as in an impressionist painting but are held discretely in place like the posters on the fence surrounding a building under construction. In Barthelme's fiction they work, not toward a revelation, but toward the apprehension of an altered reality.

Commonplace but disparate occurrences are thus brought together in what, in another context, Frank calls a "dialectic of platitude."

Though he was unhappy with the term postmodernism, which he saw linked with "metafiction," "surfiction," and "superfiction," Barthelme acknowledged it as "the least ugly, most descriptive" designation that could be applied to his fiction.[20] The qualities such fiction possesses are public rather than private, legible or hard-edged rather than soft-focused, planar rather than volumetric, committed to facsimile rather than virtuosity, finally systematic and therefore classical rather than intuitive and therefore romantic. For the modernist there is no escape from the imagination; for Barthelme no escape *except* from imagination. Paradoxically that escape relys on language, but language that is distributive or serial rather than relational, artificially composed rather than organically developed, stereotyped or repetitive rather than literary or erudite, in short not so much created as assembled. It lacks, as Charles Jencks observed of postmodern architecture, a sense of the obvious unities or, in fact, any accepted basis for signification so that, like the labyrinthine space of a Chinese garden its complex implications "always lead on to a climax that is never present . . . [and] complicate and fragment their planes and screens, non-recurrent motifs, ambiguities and jokes to suspend our normal sense of duration and extent."[21]

Perhaps the clearest visual equivalent to Barthel-

AN ADEQUATE RESPONSE TO THE WORLD

me's fiction can be seen in such postmodern structures as those of Robert Venturi, whose Guild House or whose Visiting Nurses Headquarters, like Barthelme's stories, have frequently been accused of being merely pastiche. Insisting that more was not less, Venturi issued what he termed a "gentle manifesto" which can serve equally to describe Barthelme's own practice:

I like elements which are hybrid rather than "pure," compromising rather than "clean," distorted rather than "straightforward," ambiguous rather than "articulated," perverse as well as impersonal, boring as well as "interesting," conventional rather than "designed," accommodating rather than excluding, redundant rather than simple, vestigial as well as innovating, inconsistent and equivocal rather than direct and clear. I am for messy vitality over obvious unity. I include the non sequitur and proclaim the duality.[22]

Like Venturi's ornamental layering and vernacular mannerism, Barthelme's fiction operates between contextual acknowledgment and a more neutral regard for, even an indifference to, the immediacy of its circumstances.

The equal importance accorded to each of the elements is carried into fiction in the stereotypes or parodies of classical forms embedded in the blend of gothic supernaturalism of Joyce Carol Oates, the mannered artlessness of Richard Brautigan's generic mix, the qualification of myth in Thomas Berger by the nagging details of daily life or by the plodding insistence on the logic of the ordinary in the face of insults to it. The same principle governs the substitution of verbal play for the pretense of actual history in the fiction of Stanley Elkin, Stephen Dixon, or Don DeLillo. Finally it appears in quotation or allusion to previously published material evident in the contemporary sense of appropriation, which allows artists to challenge the exclusivity of authorship. This is an age of sequels ranging from *Rocky, Friday the 13th,* and *The Godfather* in films to *Leave it to Beaver* or *The Brady Brides* on TV. No one seems to want to begin with a blank canvas.

Though they appear connected, the elements of such art remain unrelated and thus collapse upon themselves like the soft sculptures of Claes Oldenburg's icebags or typewriters, and the parallel implosion in the plots constructed by Gilbert Sorrentino's hopelessly inept authorial surrogates, interrupted monologues, or parodied styles. For Barthelme, like Sorrentino, cliché or the recognizable aspect of language becomes a device to reclaim the ordinary. Tonal no less than structural, it is this emotional neutrality that, perhaps most significantly, distinguishes Barthelme's stories from the pared-down intensities of Ernest Hemingway whose terse prose, along with that of Gertrude Stein, Barthelme's is commonly thought to resemble. In fact, Barthelme has acknowledged Hemingway as an early influence. In the absence of meaning, however, ritual for Hemingway is reduced to a compensating gesture

AN ADEQUATE RESPONSE TO THE WORLD

that gains its force by its approach to the natural world of which it is an eye witness and from which it must remain necessarily detached. Initiation is blocked rather than effected; the hero remains isolated from the community, essentially alone. Form thus outlasts and finally comes to take the place of meaning. It becomes style.

Where Hemingway's understatement relied on an underlying depth or iceberg solidity to account for the unexpressed emotion, the lack of inflection—a change in pitch or tone to indicate relationships—in Barthelme's fiction is invested with little psychological or historical density. Nothing goes on beneath events; little seems to have occurred before they are set in motion. His fiction tends toward the fixed moment rather than the flowing stream. It accords precedence to quantity over quality. It is an acknowledgment rather than a process of discovery—an acknowledgment, above all, that the narrative voice shares the attitudes and anxieties of the characters.

Barthelme's fiction is thus animated by the acceptance of action as simply part of the world rather than as a process whose unforseen rippling effect illuminates its essential nature. Such a limiting vision avoids where possible such judgmental ironies as those modernists typically used to distance themselves from the world. Kim Herzinger has identified this unease with irony in a group of writers, among whom Raymond Carver is perhaps the most prominent, who additionally share many of the minimal tendencies—limited narrative development, confined scale of the action, circumscribed tonal range—which help to define Barthelme's style:

When the 'minimalist' gives us a wan young girl, a mother puzzled by the sexual desires of her daughter, or an older man impossibly in love with a younger woman; then locates them in Cleveland, or Fort Smith, or Walla Walla; and then has them sit in a restaurant or drink Coca Cola, or go to the mall or the supermarket, or get them lost on city streets of a small midwestern town, we wait for the punchline, we expect the joke. But it doesn't come.[23]

Irony is very much a tonal element in Barthelme's fiction; but it is an element which itself proves subject to ironic challenge and which finally gives way to appreciation of the sensuous moment whose transient quality at once occasions pain and is a cause for celebration. For Barthelme, then, the joke occurs, if anywhere, in the disparity between the response the reader is prepared to make and the one the text actually invites.

Barthelme's focus on the object or on the changes it undergoes as a result of the surprising associations to which he subjects it finally emerges more in comic exhuberance than in the ironic distancing adopted by the equally small-scale or minimalist fiction with which his work has frequently been compared—the work of Ann Beattie, Raymond Carver, Grace Paley, Tobias Wolfe, or Charles Simmons, among established writers, and

AN ADEQUATE RESPONSE TO THE WORLD

that of a somewhat more recent generation identified by David Leavitt—perhaps its most prominent figure—as including Marian Thurm, Elizabeth Tallent, Peter Cameron, Meg Wolitzer, and Amy Hempel. These younger writers, Leavitt notes, "have in general limited themselves to the short story, a form they seem to find most appropriate to the age of shortened attention spans, fractured marriages and splintering families in which they grew up."[24] What this assessment suggests and what Leavitt goes on to make clear is the emergence of a new sensibility in which idealistic domestic situations give way to a more unsentimental documentation of our anxious social postures and yet a sensibility in which a consequent anger is directed "not against a way of life but against life itself." Though Barthelme's fiction struggles to reconcile these seemingly opposing attitudes—one local, the other universal—what distinguishes it from equally minimal fictions is his attempt to direct the reader to the surface of the stories rather than to identify the psychological patterns that might be said to describe the lives of his fictional characters.

The systemic experimentalism that brackets Barthelme's minimal art takes on added definition when it is set against the more visionary imagination of Cynthia Ozick, Mark Helprin, or Toni Morrison; the dreamlike reworking of mythic images in Jonathan Baumbach or Jerome Charyn; or Philip Roth's transformation of ethnic history and the family situation through which it extends its claims into the equally insistent demands of fictive expression through which the individual asserts his counterclaims. Where this maximal art finds the creative encounter lonely and ennervating, Barthelme takes delight in the inventory of the world's own energy. Where maximalism provides sharp definition for each of its voices, Barthelme often confines his figures to a single plane. Where maximalism searches for a moral as well as an esthetic reference, Barthelme refuses to validate either skepticism or belief. In maximal art, then, all situations become equally possible, for Barthelme equally impossible.

II

The omission of plot or character, even of normative dimensions of time or space in Barthelme's fiction yields a series of experimental encounters between language and reality which displaces the tensions of conventional structure. That structure is normally set in motion by a set of circumstances, that begins with a troubling imbalance someone sets out to resolve. It develops to reveal the significance of that attempt while delaying a confrontation between the central figure and someone or some force, something that works to interfere with his ambition. Finally, those opposing forces are brought to a climactic confrontation followed by a resolution which provides an assessment of its outcomes and some insight into the significance of the quarrel that brought them about.

Eliminating much of this structure, Barthelme attempts to reduce the narrative to essentials, frequently by turning to the dialogue form which, he has claimed, allowed him to deal with relationships in a pure way while providing a counter narration to the main one. "I don't have to get people in and out of doors," he explained, "I don't have to describe them. I don't have to put them in a landscape. I just deal with their voices."[25] Characteristically these stories adopt a neutral voice or remove the narrator entirely so that the dialogue is not only not subordinated to the narrative; it takes the place of narrative. Barthelme has traced these dialogues (collected largely in *Great Days*) to the example of Gertrude Stein in prose and to the pointillist technique in painting, where "what you get is not adjacent dots of yellow and blue which optically merge to give you green but merged meanings, whether from words placed side by side in a seemingly arbitrary way or phrases similarly arrayed, bushels of them. . . ."[26]

It is not only the sequence of actions that is absent from Barthelme's fictions so that there are no plots, but also the connected series of individual gestures so that there are no persons as well. As early as 1961, Barthelme noted a tendency in art toward the reemergence of the figure as a center of organization for structural elements, one that "is not placed at the service of some kind of literary 'meaning' but is, rather, enriched by anonymous human presences."[27] In his own fiction, the reference is neither exclusively to an external reality nor to an internal or imagined one. It is a world which seems to slide off the edges of the familiar so that the reader is prompted to a series of double takes as he struggles to determine which he is confronted by at a given moment. In "The Educational Experience," for example, the music which comes from somewhere to begin the story is identified as *The Semesters* by Vivaldi, a play on the eighteenth-century composer's great work, *The Seasons*. Students encounter the Fisher King at an industrial exhibit where, the reader is advised, "Transfer of information from the world to the eye is permitted if you have signed oaths of loyalty to the world, to the eye, to *Current Pathology*." The last is a text by the academic sounding team of Spurry and Entemann (the latter name, in actuality, also that of a well-known bakery) which refers to the mythic figure of the Fisher King as "a doubtful clinical entity" (*Amateurs*, 125).

Though Barthelme's fiction is dotted with brand-name references which evoke a recognizable cultural climate, it neither proposes a specific social dilemma nor provides a formal resolution to the difficulties that surface often without a dramatized cause. The details of the stories, accordingly, are grouped around disconnected and unlikely circumstances arranged in seemingly random fashion, so that even the figures themselves appear independent of or at least indifferent to them.

AN ADEQUATE RESPONSE TO THE WORLD

Barthelme's stories structurally as well as thematically address the impulse to escape from the disasters—both actual and imagined—of history or at least soften their impact. The ambiguity with which the stories treat this impulse suggests the author's sympathy for, even identification with, the desires of his characters along with his insistence on distancing himself from them. "I want to go somewhere where everything is different," complains the rich egocentric Florence Green, the title character of "Florence Green Is 81," the initial story in *Come Back, Dr. Caligari,* his first published collection. Her restlessness is echoed by the narrator Baskerville, the first of a succession of self-conscious, largely insecure writers who continue to appear in Barthelme's fiction. Baskerville attends the Famous Writers School in Westport, Connecticut, an organization that, in reality, offers only correspondence courses. Unsuccessfully attempting to interest young women, Baskerville addresses the reader directly as though speaking to a therapist whom he is, above all, afraid of boring. In an attempt to seem interesting, he mocks both the techniques of therapy and of metafiction.

As such threading in and out of reality suggests, history is not equated with actuality but is viewed as an invention which attempts to invest events with meaning or authority they do not possess, and which it proves unable to transmit. Rather than an escape into imagination, however, Barthelme's fiction depends on appearance alone as the defining element of reality.

Events are flattened so that there is no way to tell the peripheral from the central; narrative is dislocated, often shifted among varying perspectives; stories are structured on fairy-tale motifs or deal with recognizable figures of popular mythology; dissimilar story lines are juxtaposed so that the narrative is reduced to a single plane of discontinuity. Barthelme's figures move in familiar geographical or social settings but, like Jane in *Snow White*, allow one "universe of discourse" to intrude on another. Characters in a modern urban setting, for example, mix western, jive talk, and advertising jargon. Jane who is associated with Tarzan appears in the world peopled by Snow White and the dwarfs. Batman or King Kong have the same anxieties that trouble the reader. Cortés and Montezuma struggle not only with cultural perceptions but personal relationships. The vanity and ambition of the Phantom of the Opera cannot hold the attention of his author, who ultimately abandons his creation for another work all but ignored by future readers. Each of the levels of Barthelme's fictive environment, then, retains something of the reality of the others and this superimposition of unlikely qualities has the effect of blurring or double vision, resembling a photograph in which the subject moved just as the picture was being taken.

The absence either of connected movement or even internal logic further conveys what might be taken as the lack of a subject. A Barthelme story may involve a herd of porcupines who attempt to enroll at a university; a 35-year-old man unaccountably assigned to a seat in a sixth-grade classroom; a tribe of Commanches who attack a modern city; a balloon which hovers for some weeks over 45 blocks of midtown Manhattan; a noted author who makes his death into a public performance; a musician who defends his reputation by a stunning display of virtuosity; or an artist who attempts to scale a glass mountain. These occasions are made even more oblique by the absence of any clue about how to regard them. The narrative voice characteristically is deadpan, comedically refusing to acknowledge anything out of the ordinary despite the unusual, even bizarre, circumstance of his story. Backgrounds are seldom provided so that the reader is unsure who the characters are, where their conversations take place or why, or even what they are talking about. Asked by one speaker, designated solely as Q whether he is bored with the question-and-answer form, the respondent A replies, "I am bored with it but I realize that it permits many valuable omissions: what kind of day it is, what I'm wearing, what I'm thinking. That's a very considerable advantage, I would say."[28]

The advantage may be thought of, in part at least, as tactical. "Endings are elusive, middles are nowhere to be found, but worst of all is to begin, to begin, to begin," concludes the narrator of "The Dolt," (*City Life*), a story whose subject—the difficulties of art—and treatment have repeatedly caused it to be viewed as a reflection of the author's own dilemma. More significantly, however, the omissions reveal the difference between Barthelme's approach to fiction and the highly formal assumptions of modernism against which it reacts. When, as in "Daumier," (*Sadness*) an authorial surrogate sees the possibilities for an artfully constructed "situation," it is so fantastic in nature—combining several genres, among them the American western, the romantic novel of Dumas, and the contemporary customs of affluent suburbia—that it collapses upon itself to expel the figures acknowledged as imaginative into that level of fiction designated as reality. In another story from the same collection, "A City of Churches," which obliquely echoes the idealistic obsessions that often bring disaster to the characters in Hawthorne's short fiction, the perils of closure are clearly addressed in the consequences of attempting to staff a car rental agency whose incompleteness remains the one imperfection that troubles a group of otherwise smug civic leaders.

Carried over into narrative structure, such omissions give a characteristically digressive quality to Barthelme's stories that has mistakenly encouraged critics to approach them simply as a collection of fragments that reflect the dispersed quality that experience has come to have for the contemporary sensibility. The various thematic issues, the interrupted conversations, the ellipses, the parodic subject matter are not, however, incomplete parts of an overall vision; they are themselves the objects at which the author invites the reader to look. The method by which Barthelme commonly at-

AN ADEQUATE RESPONSE TO THE WORLD

tempts to incorporate these disparate elements has been described as of collage. Barthelme has himself acknowledged the central importance of collage, not only in his fiction, but in all media in the twentieth century. It is a principle whose point, he has maintained, is

that unlike things are stuck together to make, in the best case, a new reality. This new reality, in the best case, may be or imply a comment on the other reality from which it came, and may be also much else. It's an *itself*, if it's successful: Harold Rosenberg's "anxious object," which does not know whether it's a work of art or a pile of junk.[29]

What such an anxious object might also include is indicated in Barthelme's suggestion that the variety one encounters in the streets of New York might allow the city as well to be regarded as a collage. Barthelme adopts a more ironic view in one of his stories, "See the Moon" (*Unspeakable Practices, Unnatural Acts*), in which the narrator complains somewhat enviously that collage artists get away with murder.

They can pick up a Baby Ruth wrapper on the street, glue it to the canvas (in the *right place* of course, there's that), and lo! people crowd about and cry, "A real Baby Ruth wrapper, by God, what could be realer than that." Fantastic metaphysical advantage. You hate them, if you're ambitious (*UP*, 157).

UNDERSTANDING DONALD BARTHELME

Unlike the similar breakup of the object as it was projected in impressionism and subsequently in cubism in painting and in stream-of-consciousness fiction, the reductive aspect of Barthelme's ambiguous attempt to reconcile the polarities of the actual and the imaginative reflect what, Philip Stevick, speaking of Barthelme's *Snow White*, has described as the inability of form to assimilate the material out of which it is constructed.[30] That something can arbitrarily be added or taken away ensures that everything in Barthelme's collage-stories remains tentative, at once concrete in their particularity, and abstract in their overall configuration. Accordingly they might more accurately be described by a principle that the minimalist sculptor Carl Andre, speaking of his own work, has termed "anaxial symmetry."[31] The term takes its meaning from Andre's conviction that any part of a work can replace any other "like molecules in a glass of water." To resist compositional balance, Andre combines the elements of what have come to be known as his scatter pieces "according to laws which are particular to each particle, rather than a law which is applied to a whole set, like glue or riveting or welding" (55). In place of permanent bonding, then, Andre utilizes broken or preexisting parts which provide a concretized image. Such sculpture does not invite organization around a fixed point but focuses on the surface or physical mass which the spectator experiences directly by moving around and within it. "You have to really rid yourself of . . . securities and certainties and assumptions," the artist has insisted, "and get down to something which is closer and resembles some kind of blankness" (59).

This blankness, in Barthelme's fiction, emerges as a flat, two-dimensionality in which all elements are given equal weight. In "Bishop," one of the previously uncollected stories that appeared in *Sixty Stories*, a 1981 retrospective collection of his work, the rhythm mirrors the condition of the central figure on the edge of hysteria. Twice divorced and involved in an uncertain relationship with his current lover, the 49-year-old Bishop needs to establish rules specifying what hours he allows himself to have a drink throughout the day. His shaky attempt to hold onto things through liquor, long distance phone calls to friends, or by watching so much television his eyes begin to hurt seems constantly about to collapse and ultimately dissolves into a nostalgic picture of his grandparents, whose ranch he visited as a child. The story ends with Bishop's remembered image of "walking in the water, the shallow river, at the edge of the ranch, looking for minnows in the water under the overhanging trees, skipping rocks across the river, intent. . . ."[32] More than the attempt at recaptured innocence, it is the loose structure of the story which suggests its theme. Sentence follows sentence with no more explicit indication of what connects them than bulletins on the nightly news. An encounter with a child in a supermarket, excerpts from a scholarly study of a little-known American collage painter, radio programs that

Bishop listens to, the voices he hears on television commercials, and even a listing of television programs that appears in the paper are all recorded. In a typical selection the narrator notes,

> Gray in his beard, three wavy lines across his forehead. "He would frequently paint one picture over another and occasionally a third picture over the second." Frankenstein, on Peto.
> The flowers remain in their paper wrapping in the kitchen, on the butcher-block bar.
> He watches the four o'clock movie, a film he's seen possibly forty times, Henry Fonda as Colonel Thursday dancing with Sergeant Major Ward Bond's wife at the Fort Apache noncomissioned officers' ball (447).

It is Bishop's state of mind the story is concerned with; it is the loose coupling of the prose that succeeds in evoking it.

Barthelme has explictly disclaimed any interest in the kind of psychological study that would mean going beneath the surface of his characters "as if you were a Cousteau of the heart." "I'm not sure," he argues, "there's not just as much to be seen if you remain a student of the surfaces."[33] The self in his fiction accordingly becomes itself a fiction made up of endless alternatives which dissolves self-definition somewhat in the manner of a Jackson Pollock painting. The shaping boundaries of figure are dissolved into swirls or skeins or loops or nets that extend from one edge of the canvas to the other in an "all-over" composition in which every part of the painting receives equal emphasis and which thus declines to identify any dominant feature.

Unlike Pollock, however, who pictured the struggle out of which his paintings emerged, and unlike the similarly inclined metafictionists' attempt to represent the gesture of creation, Barthelme's characters are not imprisoned in their fictive environments; they are real if unsubstantial figures struggling against the ironic vision that refuses to regard them in that way. Accordingly, in a discussion that comes abruptly in the middle of "Kierkegaard Unfair to Schlegel," one speaker defensively notes that the subjective freedom irony offers substitutes an attitude for historical actuality and so not only disposes of reality but occasions only a hollow victory over the world for the ironist.

The one situation to which Barthelme keeps returning is that of the writer, the terrible cost that writing exacts, and the even more terrible fate of being unable to meet its rigorous demands. In the many stories which deal with the situation of the artist—"The Dolt," "Daumier," "The Glass Mountain," "The Flight of Pigeons from the Palace," "The King of Jazz," "Lightning," "The Great Hug," and "The Phantom of the Opera's Friend," among them—what the reader is encouraged to respond to is not, as in metafiction, the storytelling situation but the story itself, stylized rather than improvisatory and seemingly indifferent to the effort to fictionalize human behavior. Put another way, the action of Barthelme's fiction is not a function of what the characters do; it is what the language does.

This emphasis has given rise to the often overstated view that taken in its entirety the body of Barthelme's fiction reveals little development. In fact, later collections such as *Overnight to Many Distant Cities* demonstrate a deepening and ordering of experience and an expanding of fictional strategies which seem almost a necessary consequence of Barthelme's concern for language. From Florence Green's longing ("Florence Green Is 81") *to go somewhere where everything is different* and the equally plaintive desire of Snow White for "some words in the world that were not the words I always hear!" the central figures in such late stories as "Overnight to Many Distant Cities" or "Basil from Her Garden" struggle to arrive at an ecstatic appreciation of what exists around them.

Commenting as early as 1957, on the then fashionable tendency in imaginative literature in general and American theater in particular to look at human behavior in terms of psychological and sociological jargon, Barthelme noted the uneasy relation between the playwright and the psychologist.[34] Through silence, through a documentary approach influenced by postwar Italian films, and through ensemble playing, which meant that no central character emerged around whom the action focused, it was thought possible, Barthelme observed, to convey the contradictions that elude the

AN ADEQUATE RESPONSE TO THE WORLD

truths uttered in conventional speech. Such a limitation on language, Barthelme went on to argue, short-changed the audience. For one thing, it substituted for ordinary declarative speech a popular lyricism that constituted merely an inflated rhetoric. For another, it masked a system of values that presented an unbreakable determinist pattern in place of real change, revealing "the hidden outlines of a labyrinth where there are no silken threads leading back to the light" (22).

Barthelme's dissatisfaction with the notion of such a labyrinth emerged subsequently in his defence of his work along with that of other writers he identifies as postmodern, John Barth, William H. Gass, John Hawkes, Robert Coover, William Gaddis, and Thomas Pynchon, from the charge that they are preoccupied with the processes of their own writing. On the one hand he points to the need to resist the pressures of a commercial culture and of the political and sociological contamination of language by shaking words loose from their attachments in order to form new meanings, "meanings which point not toward the external world but toward the Absolute, acts of poetic intuition." Along with what, borrowing a phrase from Harold Rosenberg, he calls "the silencing of an existing rhetoric," Barthelme recognizes the correlative need to allow the particularity of the world to enter the work as, he insists, it enters our lives.[35] If renewing the language meant that content was often separated from its source or placed against a neutral background so that all objects are reduced to a sameness of contour in which it becomes impossible to determine their individual value, it also required that traces or echoes of the source be combined in often startling but at the same time familiar, patterns. Barthelme is explicit in qualifying his concern for the objectness of things. "Twenty years ago," he admits, "I was much more convinced of the autonomy of the literary object than I am now, and even wrote a rather persuasive defence of the proposition that I have just rejected: that the object is itself the world."[36] What Barthelme seems to suggest by this is the importance of not-knowing all about the subject rather than approaching it with, say, a Tolstoyan understanding. Such an approach signals the need for invention as much as discovery or, perhaps, for discovery by means of what the writer invents. But discovery of what? Of the world, certainly as much as the invention, for as Barthelme concludes, the aim of art is finally to change the world and in this attempt provide its own ethical dimension.

Barthelme's fiction, especially in its approach to language, has much in common with the cultural tendency to draw upon common art forms—the Wild West show, the music hall tradition, the comic strip—that Pauline Kael points to in her celebrated essay "Trash, Art and the Movies." The enjoyment of these films, Kael argues, comes often despite the audience's knowledge of the actors and of the circumstances in which the films are made, often, in fact, as a result of the presence

AN ADEQUATE RESPONSE TO THE WORLD

created by the actor in a series of roles in previous movies. Accordingly, she concludes, unlike pure art, movies
may be enjoyed for many reasons that have little to do
with the story or the subtleties of theme or character,
and so are more open and unlimited.[37] Kael's essay
deals for the most part with movies that came out at the
end of the sixties, a period in which she underscores the
dramatic, social, and aesthetic changes that overtook
the culture. It is also the period in which Barthelme
began to publish his stories which, significantly, appeared as did Kael's film criticism, largely in *The New
Yorker* magazine. That style is marked by a humorous
awareness which takes off not just from the way reality
has come to be seen but from the language which expresses that vision. There is a reassuring self-recogni-
tion that accompanies the characteristically ironic
judgment, so that the feeling Barthelme's stories generate is not so much that of an author's enjoyment of
himself writing as of reading what he has written.
Barthelme's parodies, then, are not of language but of
the notion that linguistic terms are static, that is, can
be confined within isolated and fixed meanings and so
control reality or alternatively establish a new aesthetic
context of their own. The sense of what Barthelme
terms "language deeply suspicious of its own behavior," and in particular the awareness of the effect of
contemporary culture on language confronts the reader
with the loss of reference and the complementary seductive nature of silence.

UNDERSTANDING DONALD BARTHELME

Barthlelme expressed his admiration for Georg Büchner's work of early modernism, *Woyzeck*, which, he notes has been called "the first modern play, the first to place the 'ordinary man' at the center of the action, the first to tear away conventional stage notions of motivations, cause, and effect."[38] The conjunction of ordinary man and the lack of motivation does, in fact, illuminate his own fictive strategy. There is no indication of how to regard the social and moral concerns of ordinary life, in fact, no way to see that such concerns affect the reader's understanding of the story. The absence of motivation, along with the absence of structural organization, is what makes the story minimal. Though Barthelme does not view cliché as redeemed through awareness, neither does he exploit for ironic purposes the difference between the actions represented and his assessment of them. Rather, as Barthelme makes clear, what it does is underscore the variety and vitality of ordinary life and the corresponding excitement of discovery that attends the attempt to express it.

Notes

1. Jo Brans, "Donald Barthelme: Embracing the World," *Southwest Review* 67 (Spring 1982). 121–37, rpt. *Listen to the Voices: Conversations with Contemporary Writers* (Dallas: Southern Methodist UP, 1988)

AN ADEQUATE RESPONSE TO THE WORLD

77–101. In addition to this source, I am indebted for much of the biographical material to J. D. O'Hara, "Donald Barthelme: The Art of Fiction LXVI," *Paris Review* 80 (1981) 180–210, and to Jerome Klinkowitz, "Donald Barthelme," *Dictionary of Literary Biography* (Detroit: Gale, 1978) 34–38.

2. O'Hara 185.

3. O'Hara 188.

4. Brans 183.

5. "After Joyce," *Location 1* (Summer 1964): 17–18.

6. Barthelme, "After Joyce" 14.

7. "Sentence," *City Life* (New York: Farrar 1970) 114. Subsequent references will be abbreviated *CL*. Other abbreviations of Barthelme's works will take the following forms: *Come Back Dr. Caligari: CB; Unspeakable Practices, Unnatural Acts: UP; Guilty Pleasures: GP; Sadness:S; Amateurs:A; Great Days:GD.*

8. "Not-Knowing," *Georgia Review* 39 (Fall 1985): 518. Alan Wilde has called attention to the ambiguous light this essay casts on Barthelme's fiction in his invaluable *Middle Grounds: Studies in Contemporary American Fiction* (Philadelphia: University of Pennsylvania Press, 1987) 165–71. I am indebted throughout this study to Wilde's readings of Barthelme's fiction, which, in addition to the source cited above may be found in more widely ranging form in *Horizons of Assent: Modernism, Postmodernism, and the Ironic Imagination* (Baltimore: Johns Hopkins UP, 1981) 166–81 and passim. In the face of near critical unanimity which finds irrealism or a fabulist impulse at the center of the postmodern imagination, Wilde recognizes a complementary realist, or as he terms it "catatonic," mode which, however, tells us something of the world's limits rather than of the choices that more conventionally have been thought to distinguish realism from naturalism. My own reading of the importance of minimalism to Barthelme's work thus differs sharply from Wilde's judgment that Barthelme belongs neither to realism nor to metafiction but remains suspensive somewhere in the middle of the two, not a distant observer but part of the world toward which he takes an ironic stance.

9. Larry McCaffery, *Anything Can Happen: Interviews with Contemporary American Novelists*, ed. Tom LeClair and Larry McCaffery (Urbana: University of Illinois Press, 1983), p. 38.

10. "Dead Men Comin' Through," *New Yorker* 1 Oct. 1979: 104.

11. "Nothing: A Preliminary Account," *Guilty Pleasures* (New York: Farrar, 1974) 165.

12. R. E. Johnson, Jr., "Bees Barking in the Night: The End and the Beginning of Donald Barthelme's Narrative," *Boundary 2*, 5 (1977) 71–92.

13. O'Hara 188.

14. O'Hara 189–90.

15. Ad Reinhardt, "Timeless in Asia," *Art News* 58 (Jan. 1960): 34–5.

16. Barthelme's remark appears in McCaffery, *Anything Can Happen* 36.

17. Alicia Legg, ed. *Sol LeWitt* (New York: Museum of Modern Art, 1978) 168.

18. Joseph Frank, "Spatial Form in Modern Literature," *The Widening Gyre: Crisis and Mastery in Modern Literature* (New Brunswick: Rutgers UP, 1963): pp. 3–62.

19. McCaffery, *Anything Can Happen*, 42.

20. McCaffery 38.

21. Charles Jencks, *The Language of Post-Modern Architecture* (New York: Rizzoli, 1984) 124.

22. Robert Venturi, *Complexity and Contradiction in Architecture*, 2nd ed.(New York: Museum of Modern Art, 1977) 16.

23. Kim Herzinger, "Introduction: On the New Fiction," *Mississippi Review* 40/41 (Winter 1985); 18.

24. David Leavitt, "New Voices and Old Values," *New York Times Book Review* May 12, 1985; 1.

25. Brans 134.

26. O'Hara 197.

27. "The Emerging Figure," *University of Houston Forum* 3 (Summer 1961); 23.

AN ADEQUATE RESPONSE TO THE WORLD

28. "The Explanation," *City Life* (New York: Farrar, 1970) 73.

29. Jerome Klinkowitz, "Donald Barthelme," in *The New Fiction: Interviews with Innovative American Writers*, ed. Joe David Bellamy (Urbana: University of Illinois Press, 1974) 52.

30. Philip Stevick, *Alternate Pleasures: Postrealist Fiction and the Tradition* (Urbana: University of Illinois Press, 1982). Citing its emphasis on verbal activity, Stevick places Barthelme's technique within the broader context of an antiformal tendency or, perhaps more accurately, a redefinition of the resources of form available in the broad range of postmodern fiction in general. I am greatly indebted to Professor Stevick for his richly suggestive comments on the first two chapters of this study.

31. Phyllis Tuchman, "An Interview with Carl Andre," *Artform* 8 (June 1970); 55–61.

32. "Bishop," *Sixty Stories* (New York: Putnam's, 1981) 449.

33. In an interview with McCaffery, *Anything Can Happen* 43.

34. "A note on Elia Kazan," *University of Houston Forum* Jan. 1957: 19–22.

35. "Not-Knowing": 513–14, 519.

36. "Not-Knowing": 521.

37. Pauline Kael, "Trash, Art, and the Movies," *Going Steady* (Boston: Little, Brown, 1970) 85–129.

38. "The Current Cinema: The Earth as an Overturned Bowl," *New Yorker* 55, 10 Sept. 1979: 120.

CHAPTER TWO

The Vernacular Isles

Barthelme has consistently mocked the modernist search for symbolic correspondence and the tendency to find in it a means a structuring art. In his first collection, *Come Back, Dr. Caligari* (1964), he introduces these themes along with a portrait of the aesthetic and spiritual exhaustion of a generation in a manner that seemed an abrupt break with the Chekhovian conventions that set the dominant form of the nineteenth- and earlier twentieth-century short story. In place of a realistic depiction of clearly defined social levels culminating in a rueful acknowledgment of the necessity of living with diminished expectations of happiness, Barthelme's fiction plunged into the chaos of contemporary experience by blending fictive and real characters, amorphous landscapes, and even levels of language and rhetorical styles, struggling all the while with its own ironies. In the absence of a conventionally agreed-upon grammar or syntax, all objects and events in Barthelme's fiction are accorded the same weight and so become virtually interchangeable. There is no dominant image, and individual elements are not discrete but subordinate to an overall pattern. The movement of words as distinct from the act of writing carries forward vestigial lexical meanings to form new and altered texts that emphasize the literal object rather than anything it may be thought to represent. Differences in meaning can be arrived at through texture, tone, rhythm, stops and starts, or modal shifts. Solidity is counterbalanced by suggestiveness, unsettling textural dislocations by repeated statement which slows and even brings to a stop the movement of time, eccentric and surprising combinations of diction by more common or recognizable lexical forms or prose rhythms, variety or ambiguity in generic types (westerns, mysteries, historical and literary parody) by a symmetry that permits the release of tensions. Along with the contradictions of linguistic environment Barthelme's stories often send the reader outside their framing reality to confront the authorial process and there encounter directly the motivation that drives the action.

This explosively discontinuous style of storytelling thus constitutes an antinarrative that is representatively illustrated in "Hiding Man." The story takes the form of a parody film thriller in which an antagonist's baffling roles and endless interpretations of them menace Burlingame, the movie-going hero. "Even Mars Bars," he is led to suspect, "have hidden significance, dangerous to plumb."[1] City life, he finds to be a "texture of mysterious noises." Like the assurance that "You can change the world," he attributes to a Catholic education, the exaggerations of horror films suggest to Burlingame a sinister intent lying just beneath the surface of ordinary experience. Even the attempt of his antagonist, Bane-Hipkiss, to move his seat in a movie theater convinces Burlingame of a hidden threat. "All life is rooted in contradiction," he insists, adding "there must be room for irony" (*CB* 27).

What troubles him about this modernist view of experience is the thought that Bane-Hipkiss may lack such concealed meaning and prove to be nothing more than he appears to be. Parodically alluding to the jargon associated with Hollywood producers, Burlingame wonders, "Where is the wienie. What happens to the twist?" What Burlingame needs to believe is that experience lends itself to the conventionally structured fictional situation, part of which gratifys the expectation of surprise. Accordingly, he continues to find in the ritual of art an echo of the mysteries promised by religion and to insist on a hidden pattern in Bane-Hipkiss's revelations. Framed alternately without subjects or finite verbs (as objects statically posed, as actions which themselves are transformed into objects), his own discourse drifts into recounted episodes of voyeurism that anticipate a device Barthelme will subsequently employ in such stories as "The Explanation" or "Kierkegaard Unfair to Schlegel." Denying ordinary events which mark the passage of time, these fevered exchanges re-

THE VERNACULAR ISLES

flect the tendency to project desire into situations that continue to frustrate its fulfillment.

In fact, Bane-Hipkiss, a self-styled "dealer in notions" does turn out to be an agent of the church masquerading as a black man, so that the irony much of the story directs toward Burlingame's suspicions turns on itself. Despite these suspicions, Burlingame insists on submitting himself to the risks inherent in ordinary experience, or at least claims he is willing to do so. Even here his claims are directed to such dramatic events as wars, plane or submarine travel, or encounters with women and are qualified by the promise, "Flight is always available, concealment is always possible" (*CB* 17). Finally, with an injection that transforms Bane-Hipkiss into a barking dog, Burlingame manages to enact a scene similar to the one he has been witnessing on the movie screen. Such evasions anticipate parallel statements in "Daumier" that there are always openings by which the self can at the very least find some distraction in fiction from the threats of everyday reality. But like that more complex story in which fiction, finally, seeks the domestic tranquility of the real, one is encouraged in "Hiding Man" to accept both the world and the criticism to which fiction subjects its illusions. "One believes what one can," Burlingame concludes, "follows the vision which most brilliantly exalts and vilifies the world" (*CB* 35).

Exaltation and vilification of the world alternate in

"For I'm the Boy Whose Only Joy Is Loving You," which deals with the attempts of a character named Bloomsbury to deal with his recent separation from his wife. Bloomsbury, whose name evokes the preoccupation with states of consciousness that characterized the writing of a London literary group of the twenties, struggles, among other things, to reconcile his actual responses with the feelings expected of him. His two friends, Huber and Whittle express a vicarious curiosity about his reaction to the divorce and, in particular, about the details of the custody or property settlement. "Who got the baby if there was a baby," they wonder, "what food remains in the pantry at this time, what happened to the medicine bottles including Mercurochrome, rubbing-alcohol, aspirin, celery tonic, milk of magnesia, No-Doz, and Numbutal . . ." (*CB* 60). Where Whittle adopts the formal manner of a legal document, Huber confines his understanding to lexical terms. A bachelor, he defends his challenge to Whittle's description of the pain of divorce with the assertion that "I may not know about marriage . . . but I know about words" (CB, 61). In either case, while the standard form of their questions generalize Bloomsbury's life so that it is indistinguishable from that of any other, the detailed specificity gives their inquiry a life of its own.

In his wife, Martha, Bloomsbury encounters the displacement of feeling by words. She would rather read (she is engrossed in a volume of Mallarmé) than respond to his sexual overtures. To compensate, he invents a Walter Mitty-like fantasy of a seductive Irish cyclist named Pelly, who responds more enthusiastically. Even this reverie, occurring intermittently in the story and introduced without transitions, is constructed in a dialect whose form resembles the stylistic parodies James Joyce embedded in *Ulysses*. Once physical separation is transformed into language, Bloomsbury realizes, "The question is not what is the feeling but what is the meaning?" (*CB* 61).

This ambivalent attitude toward language surfaces in the clichéd expressions ("steely eyes") including those adverbial dialogue tags ("Huber said 'bitterly'") which Barthelme italicizes or encloses in quotation marks to indicate an awareness of their imitative function and consequent lack of force. The awareness, however, invests these terms with renewed if ironic energy so that even the title of the story is drawn from a line in a popular song and in a slapstick scene in which the two friends beat Bloomsbury about the head first with a bottle then with a tire iron, he is made to express his feeling in tears as well as in "all sorts of words."

It is, in fact, the demand made upon the media for words and images that will compensate for the emotional sterility that gives ironic point to the title for the entire volume, a title Barthelme drew from the German expressionist film *The Cabinet of Dr. Caligari*. Barthelme's story "The Big Broadcast of 1938" contains the only allusion to that source (other than the inclusion of Caligari's name in a listing of real and fictitious doctors in "Up,

Aloft in the Air"), in an oblique reference to the star of the German silent film, Conrad Veidt, who is said by a movie fan to represent a vital part of her imagination.

In the story, Bloomsbury, now divorced, has obtained a radio station as part of the divorce settlement. His broadcasts are limited to repetitions either of "The Star-spangled Banner" or of words that appeal to him, such as "nevertheless" or "matriculate," which, when repeated in a monotonous voice for as long as minutes "disclose new properties, unsuspected qualities" (*CB* 68). Addressed to the public, these messages contrast with a second type of broadcast described as commercial announcements which take the form of appeals to his ex-wife, Martha, whose habit had been to post the subject of their quarrels on the notice board at breakfast.

Bloomsbury adopts the same banalities both in language and situation he believes represent the cultural norms to nostalgically remind Martha of incidents in their life together. "I was, in a sense," he explains at one point, "an All-American boy" (*CB* 76) and later explains that meant he was married. At the same time, while he constantly qualifies these expressions by an awareness that they only approximate reality, he continues to amass a catalog of clichés that reflect the images given to society by the media in place of individually perceived experience. At one point, for example, Bloomsbury responds to a sexual invitation with a self-consciousness even the narrative is made to echo. "With a single stride, such as he had often seen practiced in the films," the reader is instructed, "Bloomsbury was 'at her side'" (*CB* 79).

Ultimately these clichés serve to establish a reality of their own. In a typical description Bloomsbury recalls

that remarkable day, that day unlike any other, that day, if you will pardon me, of days, on that old day from the old days when we were, as they say, young, we walked if you will forgive the extravagance *hand in hand* into a theatre where there was a film playing (*CB* 70).

The choice of a movie theater is, once again, strategic, both evoking their feelings and mocking the literary pretentiousness which both describes, and even in part accounts for, it. Some tentative sexual overtures Bloomsbury makes seem less interesting to him than the film they are watching and as they sit in the balcony, the smoke from the cigarettes below smells to them "like the twentieth century." When Martha, apparently touched by Bloomsbury's commercials, does offer a reconciliation, however, he retreats to the aptly named control room of his station, only to find that isolated from the everyday world of bill paying and domestic quarrels he is cut off (in this case by the electric company) from the source of energy needed to broadcast.

The pressures of corporate life and the breakup of a marriage have compensatory as well as punitive consequences in "Me and Miss Mandible," in which

UNDERSTANDING DONALD BARTHELME

Joseph, a 35-year-old insurance adjustor unaccountably finds himself assigned a seat in a fourth-grade classroom. "I take the right steps, obtain correct answers," Joseph abruptly blurts out near the end of the story, "and my wife leaves me for another man" (*CB* 110). Though his anomalous presence in the classroom merely literalizes his wife's judgement that he is a child, Joseph's teacher, Miss Mandible, like his classmates, accepts it without remark. In fact he becomes the object of both his teacher's sexual interest and that of his classmate Sue Ann Brownley, who although only eleven is "clearly a woman, with a woman's disguised aggression and a woman's peculiar contradictions" (*CB* 98). In a complaint that echoes the unfocused feeling of his generation, Joseph observes, "Only I, at times (only at times), understand that somehow a mistake has been made, that I am in a place where I don't belong" (*CB* 98).

Compelled by his former profession to assess the "debris of our civilization," Joseph sees the world as a vast junkyard comprised of potential fragments, part of which, in the form of various written records (diplomas, membership cards, marriage licenses, insurance forms, Army discharge papers) he relied on to establish his identity. "I confused authority with life itself" (*CB* 102) he concludes. Employing a device that will become a staple of Barthelme's fiction, Joseph recites a litany of the class roll, the solidity of names standing in sharp relief to the activity in which he is engaged and which reminds him of his Army experience where "much of

THE VERNACULAR ISLES

what we were doing was absolutely pointless, to no purpose" (*CB* 98). The pointlessness of authority proves as much cultural as institutional. Joseph recognizes in a popular movie magazine the exaggerated models which control society's expectations and at the same time ensure the inability to fulfill them. "Signs are signs," Joseph realizes, "and some of them are lies" (*CB* 109).

The reliance on social signs similarly informs the stylistic experiments Barthelme employs in "The Viennese Opera Ball," which sets the pattern for Barthelme's collage stories. Without any narrative structure or overriding action that would account for motivation of the characters or provide an environment in which their several histories can be contained or subordinated, the story lists the guests both attending and absent from a fashionable social event. Around this listing Barthelme strings a series of verbal pyrotechnics (puns, word games, obscure facts, technical references). Conversations are overheard, careers of the guests are rehearsed, gossip exchanged touching on subjects ranging from obstetrics to corporate strategies and including material from slick magazines as well as an index to a book on Dostoevsky. Like the many lists which subsequently appear in Barthelme's fiction, those in "The Viennese Opera Ball" have little in common. The references are not, as in collage, juxtaposed to imply some relation or to arrive at some unsuspected unity but are allowed to exist next to one another like the tenants in an apartment building. What justifies their grouping is solely the forced relation to the ball. While this placement subverts any attempt at intimacy, it does restore a tangible reality to words by connecting them to things rather than to interpretations or ideas about things.

The non sequitur also constitutes the compositional principle of "Up, Aloft in the Air" and "The Joker's Greatest Triumph" which parody comic-strip melodrama, often by transforming exaggerated heroics and metaphorical expressions into literal events. Such parody in Barthelme's fiction is directed not only toward literary expression but also the cultural willingness to take the forms of its feeling from literary images. In "A Shower of Gold," the final story in *Come Back, Dr. Caligari* and one of Barthelme's most frequently anthologized pieces, Peterson, a largely unsuccessful artist sees an opportunity to make some money by appearing on a television quiz program called "Who Am I?" in which the host prods the contestants to acknowledge the absurd as the defining condition of their identity. Interviewed by Miss Arbor, one of the program's production staff, Peterson is told the nature of the program: "Man stands alone in a featureless, anonymous landscape, in fear and trembling and sickness unto death. God is dead. Nothingness is everywhere. Dread. Estrangement. Finitude. *Who Am I?* approaches these problems in a root radical way" (*CB* 174). Though Peterson initially expresses some reservations about his belief in the absurd, his own art reflects something of its nature. Combining "three auto radiators, one from a Chevrolet

THE VERNACULAR ISLES

Tudor, one from a Ford pickup, one from a 1932 Essex, with part of a former telephone switchboard and other items," his art is, in its brand names, its eclectic references, its seeming lack of order or coherence, somewhat suggestive of Barthelme's own stories. Not surprisingly, it doesn't sell and Peterson is advised to saw the work in half by his dealer, who characterizes Peterson's notion of the integrity of art as a romantic idea. "You read too much in the history of art," Peterson is advised by the dealer, who also adopts the jargon of existential philosophy. "It estranges you from those possibilities for authentic selfhood that inhere in the present century" (*CB* 175).

Peterson's philosophy as well as his art find an ironic echo in the abrupt appearance in his studio of a man carrying a switchblade who identifys himself as a cat-piano player and who in fact literalizes a criticsm commonly made of avant garde music by producing an instrument made of cats from which he proceeds to extract shrill, discordant sounds. Like everyone else, he speaks in phrases drawn from existential philosophy. "Choices, Mr. Peterson, choices," he points out of a kitten that wandered into the studio, "You *chose* that kitten as a way of encountering that which you are not, that is to say, kitten. An effort on the part of the *pour-soi* to—" (*CB* 179).

Peterson is finally brought to acknowledge the absurdity of life after a series of events which suggest society's rejection of his art as well as its misapprehensions of the life of an artist. Even Peterson's barber, whose conversation is filled with references to Nietzsche and to Martin Buber's analysis of the I-Thou relation and who has himself written four books all titled *The Decision to Be,* feels qualified to judge his efforts while in a surrealistic episode, the President arrives with a contingent of Secret Service men to destroy Peterson's sculpture. When shortly afterward three girls from California move into his loft (a situation Barthelme will return to as the basis for his novel *Paradise*) quoting Pascal and preparing dishes called *veal engagé,* Peterson agrees to appear on the television show. Once there he finds that the master of ceremonies (who at first appears to resemble the President of his fantasies) uses a polygraph to determine the validity of the contestants' responses which, when judged inauthentic, are exposed as being in BAD FAITH in huge glowing letters.

Once again, Barthelme alludes to the questionable accuracy of signs. Though now willing to acknowledge the absurdities of modern urban life (another of which he identifies in a sign that reads "Coward Shoes" in ten-foot letters), Peterson nonetheless resists the idea that they necessarily define existence or that they must shape the character of his art. "Don't be reconciled," he desperately cautions the audience, "Turn off your television sets . . . cash in your life insurance, indulge in a mindless optimism. Visit girls at dusk. Play the guitar" (*CB* 183). To confirm this philsophy of eclectic risk, Peterson insists on the mythic background of his own identity. "My mother" he announces, "was a royal virgin . . . and my father a shower of gold" (*CB* 183). A narrative voice indicates how these remarks are to be taken. "Peterson went on and on," the story concludes, "and although he was, in a sense, lying, in a sense he was not" (*CB* 183). The description of Peterson's somewhat feverish appeal for spontaneity suggests that one danger lies in a loss of control. The result is an ambivalence which surfaces in the urgencies of the cat-piano player, who utters the banalities of existential jargon but whose discordant music resembles that of Barthelme's. It is through that music that the story conveys the sense in which Peterson is, at length, finally not lying—the revelation of the magical qualities, that despite all logic to the contrary remain embedded in ordinary experience.

In *Unspeakable Practices, Unnatural Acts,* Barthelme's second collection of stories, the concentration on the sixties preoccupation with alienation broadens into a concern for sexual and marital tensions and the awareness of the abstractions of fiction or, more accurately, its attempt to connect events into a coherent pattern as distinct from the concrete immediacy of language. Both of these themes inform "The Indian Uprising," the initial story in the volume and justly one of the most celebrated in Barthelme's canon. The issues that prompt the uprising are difficult to identify with any certainty, and in fact the adherents to each side and the principles for which they stand continue to shift. "Which side are you on?" characters continue to demand of each other, recalling the slogans that marked the labor-management battles of the thirties. One war, Barthelme seems to suggest is pretty much like another. The most comprehensive of these turns out to be the war between the sexes which appears to take place at least in part as a film or, more accurately, as several films in which the camera moves from set to set or around sets drawn principally from the Second World War. Against the passion of the Commanche Indians who attempt to storm a city, the narrator erects barricades of impersonality constructed of doors he has built over an extended period of domestic battles with various women. Additionally these barricades consist of a disparate collection of objects including ashtrays, corkscrews, bottles of wine and liquor, blankets, musical instruments, and job descriptions. None of these affords the narrator any insight into the nature of the conflict ("I decided I knew nothing," he admits) or into the personal dilemma echoed in the nervousness of the city itself which "does not know what it has done to deserve baldness, errors, infidelity" (*UP* 6).

The view the reader obtains of the narrator's life is thus partial; his background is never fully presented, his motives remain asserted rather than accounted for. Even the outlines of the city that serves as the setting for the story remain sketchy and neither help to explain nor influence events. In place of narrative development the story itself is an exposition of the narrator's motives

THE VERNACULAR ISLES

and focuses on his attempt to capture a woman named Sylvia, a porno film actress whose bear-claw necklace and shrill cries associate her with the attacking Indians. "It is you I want now," the narrator tells her, "here in the middle of this Uprising." Later he admits that "The sickness of [their] quarrel lay thick in the bed" (*UP* ll). What the narrator identifies as the history of the heart is shortly followed by a history of torture, which he relates to a friend significantly called Block, and as the battle goes on the narrator grows more and more drunk as he grows more and more in love.

While Sylvia remains indifferent, the narrator is ambiguously consoled by a schoolteacher identified only as Miss R., an instructor in counterinsurgency. Plain in appearance, clinical in manner, Miss R. alternately insults him and expresses the most intimate endearments. Initially identified with the barricade of words behind which the narrator fights off the attack, Miss R. resists the "unpleasant combinations" that she attributes to the nature of society but that emerge in the many literary allusions that mark the narrative as well as in its overall compositional strategy. "You gave me heroin first a year ago," Sylvia tells the narrator, in a play on T. S. Eliot's reference to a gift of hyacinths in *The Waste Land*. When one Commanche is captured, he identifies himself as Gustave Aschenbach, the central figure of Thomas Mann's "Death in Venice," a study of repressed passion and unrequited love. Though she quotes Valéry, Miss R. more conservatively discourages such suggestive parallels. "I believe," she explains, "our masters and teachers as well as plain citizens should confine themselves to what can be safely said" (*UP* 8–9).

What can be safely said proves to be the "hard, brown, nutlike word," in which, Miss R. insists, there is enough aesthetic excitment . . . to satisfy anyone but a damned fool" (*UP* 9). Accordingly, the only form of discourse she approves of is the litany, which she illustrates as a list of words with no apparent connection whether they are organized into a horizontal collage or a vertical hierarchy. In what has often been taken as Barthelme's own view, the narrator goes even further to claim that "strings of language extend in every direction to bind the world into a rushing, ribald whole" (*UP* 11). What the story conveys, while undeniably ribald, is less cohesive, and at the end the narrator is made to surrender even those accessories that hold things together, such as his belt and shoelaces. Binding the world moreover carries a sense of confinement or restriction which, despite his resolve to remain nonevaluative in responding to Miss R., the narrator underscores in his puritannical disapproval of his friend Jane's adulterous relationship. In contrast to the cohesive power the narrator attributes to language, then, the narrative itself advances from one subject to the next in a more abrupt, cinematic manner. Pictures follow other pictures without explanation or warning. Commenting on Miss R.'s remarks, for example, the narrator suddenly shifts the reference of a pronoun to begin talking about the Commanches:

Then they pulled back in a feint near the river and we rushed into that sector with a reinforced battalion hastily formed among the Zouaves and cabdrivers. This unit was crushed in the afternoon of a day that began with spoons and letters in hallways and under windows where men tasted the history of the heart, cone-shaped muscular organ that maintains *circulation of the blood* (*UP* 6).

Though the emphasis on the technical aspect of workings of the heart concludes the passage with what might be an entry from a scientific manual, what is reaffirmed is the principle of fluidity. The narrator finds himself literally thrown from one situation to another. At length even Miss R. is revealed to belong to the party of the Commanches, whose "savage black eyes, paint, feathers, beads" all suggest feminine makeup and costume. Feeling triumphs over the attempt at structure. Men are betrayed by women. Art capitulates to life.

The sudden shifts in narrative focus and the resistance to thematic closure that such shifts indicate similarly structure "The Balloon," which describes the sudden appearance above forty-five blocks in midtown Manhattan of a balloon whose amorphous shape and obscure origin suggest unmistakable parallels with

Barthelme's own fiction. The balloon is multicolored, anchored to the ground at various points by a number of sliding weights, and distinguished by a deliberate lack of finish, which imparts to the surface a "rough, forgotten quality." Even the point of entry is concealed, making the balloon all but inaccessible to ordinary citizens, who are made uncomfortable by this interference with their vision of a familiar reality. Above all, it does not lend itself to conventional structuring of events. "It is wrong, the reader is warned, "to speak of 'situations' implying sets of circumstance leading to some resolution, some, escape of tension; there were no situations, simply the balloon hanging there" (*UP* 16). Appropriately, arguments about the meaning of the balloon soon end, the narrator goes on to explain, "because we have learned not to insist on meanings, and they are rarely even looked for now, except in cases involving the simplest, safest phenomena" (*UP* 16). What was important, the reader learns, in a statement that directs the response Barthelme seems to encourage for all fiction as well, "was what you felt when you stood under the balloon" (*UP* 19).

The appearance of the balloon nonetheless invites a variety of reactions from the public and critics alike, a "flood of original ideas in all media," the narrator drily observes, which constitute "works of singular beauty as well as significant milestones in the history of inflation" (*UP* 16). The comic offsetting of that final "history of inflation" indicates to the reader how Barthelme wants such interpretations viewed. But to make certain, the narrator concludes by dismissing all generalizations. "At that moment," he points out, "there was only *this balloon*, concrete particular, hanging there" (*UP* 16).

The playfulness which allows Barthelme to randomly juggle the words, plot lines, and levels of reality finds a corresponding expression in the less intellectual reactions the balloon occasions which range from hostility to pleasure. Against the increasingly rigid complexities of modern urban life, one of which, the narrator suggests, makes questionable the desirability of long-term commitments, the balloon, in its randomness offers the possibility of "mislocation of the self."

The slyly ironic comment on long-term commitments betrays an attitude Barthelme frequently adopts toward marriage in his fiction. The lack of definition, however, is itself qualified by the tendency people have to locate themselves in relation to those intersections where the balloon touches reality, at which points it becomes possible to turn "in a flash from old exercises to new exercises, risks and escalations." The story demonstrates such an abrupt thematic shift when, at the conclusion, the narrator accepts responsibility for the balloon, which he reveals finally as a "spontaneous autobiographical disclosure" through which he attempted to compensate for the loneliness and sexual deprivation he feels at the absence of a lover. The sudden appearance of the narrator undercuts what fictive conviction the largely plotless story had previously gen-

erated, and, since the disclosure adds one more disparate element, it is probably better not to take too literally
either the spontaneity or the autobiography. What does
emerge as the central concern of the story is the suggestive contradictions of art that remain to be experienced
rather than interpreted and that point to the variety and
excitement that lie not within the depth but ready-to-
hand on the surface where art and experience intersect.

Art proves similarly disappointing as a means of
interpreting its subject in "Robert Kennedy Saved from
Drowning," in which the narrator records his observations about Kennedy, describes episodes in his life, and
provides snatches of conversation or statements he is
supposed to have made. Each of the segments is given
its own heading; none is accorded more importance
than any of the others. They do not build toward some
definitive revelation or in their totality establish a definitive portrait. Collectively they serve more as a catalog
than a coherent perspective from which to view their
subject. Like the balloon, Kennedy proves more various, more surprising, even mysterious, finally capable
of wide ranges of behavior which seem impossible to
reconcile. Gracious as an employer, attentive as a husband and father, compassionate even as a child, he can
be abrupt and insensitive, both assured and vulnerable.
Though partial to soberly cut suits in dark colors, he is
pictured, at length, with a mask, black cape, and sword.
This romantic notion is reinforced by Kennedy's large-
scale ambitions which, however moral, seem hopelessly

THE VERNACULAR ISLES

naïve. "The world is full of unsolved problems," he is quoted as saying, "situations that demand careful reason and intelligent action. In Latin America, for example" (*UP* 44). The example is so arbitrary, so unfocused, above all so inadequate in its lack of specificity that Kennedy's pronouncement along with the flat, terse assertions he is constantly quoted as uttering make him seem almost a cartoonlike figure of authorial mockery.

Yet Kennedy himself provides a paradigm for responding to the fiction in his erudite discussion of the French writer Georges Poulet's analysis of the eighteenth-century French dramatist Pierre Marivaux. Quoting Poulet, Kennedy identifies a figure he terms the Marivaudian being:

A pastless futureless man, born anew at every instant. The instants are points which organize themselves into a line, but what is important is the instant, not the line. The Marivaudian being has in a sense no history. Nothing follows from what has gone before. He is constantly surprised. He cannot predict his own reaction to events. He is constantly being *overtaken* by events. A condition of breathlessness and dazzlement surrounds him. In consequence he exists in a certain freshness which seems, if I may say so, very desirable (*UP* 46).

Frustrating linear definition, the historical understanding of what follows from the knowledge of what has gone before, the Marivaudian figure perhaps best describes the story itself; yet part of the disturbing effect the story has is the dissatisfaction it projects with its own approach. Reducing Kennedy to the Kafkaesque near invisiblity of the letter *K*, the narrator in the manner of overstuffed biographies in which the subject is figuratively drowned also includes such trivial information as the exact dishes he has ordered in a restaurant or the word-for-word text of an alphabet lesson he read to his children and includes a digressive passage describing the indifferent young people who line the streets along which Kennedy walks.

As in "The Balloon," the story concludes with the intrusive appearance of the narrator, who emerges to dramatically rescue Kennedy from an unexplained drowning and thus, once more, shifts from conflict between the characters to that between them and a formerly distant observer. Bringing Kennedy onto firm ground, the narrator receives only terse, noncommital thanks, which suggests both the importance fictive characters place on independence from their author and the dangers to which it subjects them.

In "The Dolt," the narrator shares the difficulties of Edgar, who in several attempts has been unable to pass the National Writers' Examination and so earn a certificate which will allow him to write for the leading periodicals. Although he has no trouble with the oral part, Edgar ironically confesses, it is the written which gives him the most difficulty. Edgar struggles as well within a strained marriage. His ambitious wife, who is

THE VERNACULAR ISLES

described as sexually attractive but very mean, turns her back on him and, while secretly hoping to be dominated, remains faintly contemptuous of his ability. Edgar's domestic situation is further aggravated by the appearance of his son "who was eight feet tall and wore a serape woven out of two hundred transistor radios, all turned on and tuned to different stations" (*UP* 69), who leans over his parents "like a large blaring building" impatiently demanding to know whether they have any marijuana. Edgar's pedantic manner and the artificial approach he adopts toward his writing—he deliberately uses archaic words to make his stories seem more interesting—contribute to his dilemma. His principal difficulty, however, is his lack of talent. His unintentionally parodic style is labored and imitative, marked by convoluted prose and intricate, melodramatic plots whose structure, much like Barthelme's, is often digressive and lacks conventional development. At the conclusion of the story the authorial association becomes explicit with the intrusion of the narrator to admit that he, too, has the same problems.

The difficulties experienced by the writer, the worst of which according to the intrusive narrator of "The Dolt" is "to begin, to begin, to begin," are "In A Picture History of the War" extended to the difficulty of being understood. The war referred to in the title is between fathers and sons, a conflict that here receives a preliminary treatment Barthelme will subsequently expand in

The Dead Father. The story begins surrealistically with the young Kellerman running drunkenly "through the park at noon with his naked father slung under one arm." Formerly a general whose mythic stature is suggested by the battles he claims to have fought throughout history, the older Kellerman is reduced to the helplessness that comes with age and the disappointments it brings particularly in his hopes for his son who has becomes not a warrior as his father hoped but a bridge expert ("the father of a book on the subject," he boasts). What the general laments the most, however, is the loss of authority. Confessing his fear of advancing age which, he notes, along with guilt, "mess up the real world of objects," he comically identifies his feeling of superfluousness in his lack of familiarity with the sound of contemporary jazz. Unfamiliar with the critical terms in which it is described, he asks plaintively:

Why does language subvert me, subvert my seniority, my medals, my oldness, whenever it gets a chance? What does language have against me—me that has been good to it, respecting its little peculiarities and nicilosities, for sixty years? (*UP* 139–40).

The father's complaint disolves finally into a series of questions that resemble those a child might ask ("Where does 'hair' go when it dies?") and, so echo rather than respond to the uncertainties his own son expresses. Faced with his father's inadequacy, the

younger Kellerman, at length, turns for answers to surrogates, first the popular social critic Paul Goodman,
then a fireman, both of whom serve as alternate models
of childlike hero-worship. Neither father nor son speak
the same language. Each confesses his own weakness
in a babble of double-talk so that what the story finally
addresses is the breakdown of language. "There are
worms in words," the general exclaims bitterly, comparing their movement to that of Mexican jumping beans
which are "agitated by the warmth of the mouth" (*UP*
142). For his son, the father's combination of helplessness and arbitrary exercise of power along with the desirability of mothers remain a troubling mystery, and
as he continues literally to run after answers he passes
a nominally heroic cluster of firemen who, it turns out,
know little more than even he does about fires and
stand around in confusion asking questions of each
other.

The attempt to hold things together in the absence
of meaningful connections emerges in two complementary stories, "Edward and Pia," and "A Few Moments
of Sleeping and Waking," both of which adopt a style
of monotonously declarative sentences, often repetitive
in content as well, to mirror the empty relationship of
an expatriate couple. In "Edward and Pia," they move
across the neutral landscape of several European cities,
worrying about money, desperate for company, and
quarreling about whether to separate. Though Edward
finds it necessary to defend his country against its in-

volvement in Vietnam and the violence of American culture that culminates in the assassination of President Kennedy, neither Pia's Swedish family nor the European society in which they travel seem more appealing. Unmarried, the pregnant Pia continues to reject Edward's sexual overtures while he retreats to scheduled reading in popular magazines and to drinking as an escape from the instability of their lives.

The aimlessness and boredom of their relationship, which ultimately borders on hysteria, turns in "A Few Moments of Sleeping" to a self-examination the couple conducts mainly through the interpretation of their dreams. The intricate analyses, some of which reveal the tension between Pia and her mother, are called into question by the equal reliance Edward places on Freud's *The Interpretation of Dreams* and on *Madam Cherokees' Dream Book*. The image of Edward smoking a cigar further undercuts the authority of interpretation by its suggestion of the celebrated comment Freud made to his daughter that sometimes a cigar is just a cigar. Finally though Edward decides his interest in discovering Pia's dark side has led him to regard her as a moon, he continues to find in popular images a means of projecting his own situation and drunkenly becomes upset by her mistaken description of the film *Mrs. Miniver*. Disappointed with what her dreams reveal, Pia assures herself they have no significance. She rejects even the form they take and in attempting to control even her dreams, indicates something of the quirky determination and

THE VERNACULAR ISLES

resolute sense of purpose Barthelme's men find so difficult to deal with.

In "See the Moon," the concluding story of *Unspeakable Practices, Unnatural Acts*, the difficulty of both artistic and social communication is focused in the hostility expressed both by and toward the conventional symbol of romance. "See the moon?" an expectant father warns his as yet unborn child, "it hates us" (*UP* 156). Though he devotes himself to what he calls lunar hostility studies, the narrator is never specific about what the moon represents or the reasons for its hostility. The contrast between the difficulty he experiences finding some pattern or sense of continuity in his life and the more imaginative quality with which he hoped as a young man to invest it suggests that his judgment of the moon is, at least in part, ironic.

The narrator's attempts to organize his experience into some meaningful arrangement are frustrated by the indiscriminate proliferation of facts not only in his own history but as they must appear as well to his son's generation, one of whom, he feels, must be overwhelmed by the relentless number of siblings his parents list on a school membership roll. His search for meaning takes the form of identifying the significant details of his history and leads the narrator to mount a random selection of objects associated with his career on a bulletin board. They range from a cardinal's red hat (signifying his struggles with religious conviction) to a traffic ticket issued while he worked at a meaningless job doing public relations for the president of a university. "Fragments," he explains of his holding onto these objects, "are the only forms I trust." The statement has so universally been taken as an expression of the author's own esthetic that Barthelme felt obliged in one interview to explictly if comically repudiate it.[2]

Determined to serve as a "sort of Distant Early Warning System" for his yet unborn child, what the narrator suggests is a suspicion of "the knowledgeable knowers knowing." Fragmentation is thus not meant to serve as a trustworthy guide to dealing with diminished possibility in the future so much as it represents a more realistic way of assessing the narrator's past idealistic and grandiose schemes. The narrator comes closer to Barthelme's intention in his admission that the bulletin board "souvenirs," as he calls them, will "someday merge, blur—cohere is the word, maybe—into something meaningful," something, he goes on to explain, that will be looked at as a work of art.

"Is there any value that has value?" he demands of a friend, identifed only as Cardinal Y. "If there is," he is advised, "then it must lie outside the sphere of what happens" (*UP* 167). An enigmatic figure, the cardinal confirms the shallowness of religious answers to the troubling questions the narrator puts to him. He seldom ventures beyond a depth of ten inches, the reader is told, and regards as significant the color and material out of which his gloves are made. At the same time he

THE VERNACULAR ISLES

deftly and with some gaiety eludes the narrator's heavy-handed and humorless attempts to probe the sources of his belief, attempts which receive an "odd blessing" from the cardinal but which reveal little about the moon and provide only a limited basis for understanding cardinals. "One can measure and measure," the narrator realizes, "and miss the most essential thing" (*UP* 168).

Like the color-field painters, who attempted to eliminate the illusion of depth by reproducing the edge of the canvas within the boundaries of the picture plane to remind the viewer of the flatness of the painting, Barthelme once again allows the narrator to interrupt the story by commenting directly on its progress. Columbus, he recalls, was concerned about sailing off the edge of the globe. His own literary voyages are much less heroically conceived in terms of folding paper airplanes, the concern for whose contours prompts the narrator to remark, "Show me a man who worries about edges and I'll show you a natural-born winner" (*UP* 156). Subsequently after announcing his intention to present one of the characters only in outline, he urges the reader not to lose interest, promising to introduce such spectacular events as a greased-pig chase and (with perhaps an inadvertent nod in the direction of the story that Barthelme devoted to just such an event) a balloon launching.

The difficulty he experiences in arriving at coherence is underscored in his attempt to explain to his second wife, Ann, the awkwardness and sense of responsibility the anticipated birth of their child occasions and also in a series of abrupt telephone conversations he has with his son Gregory, whose own restlessness the narrator feels responsible for. Gregory's sporadic interest in family history does not affect his intention to pursue a career in science rather than, as his father humorously advises, explore the "Vernacular Isles." The term "vernacular" suggests an interest in the colloquial or immediate rather than the merely literary and the narrator acknowledges that what led to the his divorce from his first wife, Sylvia, was his habit of moonstaring as an everyday activity.

It is these ordinary pursuits—the sphere of what happens—the narrator finally settles for, which is not to say the conventional ones, such as those opinions the Cardinal holds about the moon. Instead the narrator contents himself with viewing the "Sea of Tranquility" through the screened grid of a porch, admires the civilized art of Max Beerbohm's satiric drawing, and settles back to wait for the delivery man wearing a green siren suit, red-faced and with a blond shaved head, to drive up in an orange and blue Gulf Oil truck with kerosene for his space heater. The rainbow colors suggest something of the vividness with which the ordinary scene strikes the narrator making somewhat ambivalent the irony with which he describes the exchange of clichés with the driver as a "rich verbal transaction." To compensate, the narrator unfolds figures of the imagination which, along with his history and memories and the attempt to integrate them into some comprehensive and definitive statement, he associates with the moon. Against that harsh influence and animosity he warns his as yet unborn child.

City Life, Barthelme's third collection of short stories, made even more apparent the author's break with the conventional short story of psychological inwardness—the examination of character and incident leading to some usually sudden epiphany or revelation. It is the writer who chooses which word, which sentence, will follow the next, not the logic of the story. Boldfaced headings provide a choral accompaniment to the text. Mock engravings do not illustrate the stories but serve as their subject, reducing the text to captions. Sentences dissolve into fragments of thought, which—as in the curiously disjointed "Bone Bubbles"—are presented without punctuation in a stream of consciousness that links unlikely associations to constitute "misrecognitions of the ego." Narrative gives way to what seems like meditation or verbal display and to a foregrounding of fiction which does not, as in metafiction, undercut the validity of the text but merges it in surprising combinations.

No longer content simply to mirror events, Barthelme abandons the formal structure that separates the fictive world from the real. The factual is mingled with what is invented, and both are presented in a straight-faced tone that deprives the reader of any clues to enable him to tell the difference. New realities con-

UNDERSTANDING DONALD BARTHELME

tinue to displace old ones. Accordingly Barthelme's stories seldom provide the feel of a completed statement or answered question. Though references are frequently drawn from contemporary urban experience, neither form nor content remain fixed or, for that matter, known. The concerns of the volume range beyond its anxieties to include the imaginative possibilities that bring art, and in particular language, closer to and allow it to shape life.

In "Views of My Father Weeping," the initial story in the collection, the unsettling image of a father's tears continues to haunt the son's ineffectual efforts to discover who was responsible for his death. Contradictory information continues to pile up which alternately reveals the father as an embarrassing clown childishly jamming his thumb into a tray of cupcakes, a stern disciplinarian, and a self-pitying drunkard. Even the accident which led to his death proves subject to varying interpretations depending on which witness is consulted. Like the similarly disconnected episodes of "Robert Kennedy Saved from Drowning," the conflicting information prevents the narrator from arriving at any clear picture of his father and the story ends with "Etc." suggesting the evidence, no item of which is more important than any other, might be accumulated indefinitely without bringing the search to a conclusion.

The conflict between fathers and sons is treated again in "At the Tolstoy Museum," where, as Jochen

THE VERNACULAR ISLES

Achilles points out, the architecture of the museum stands as an expression of Tolstoy's literary as well as moral authority which, the narrator is afraid, appears constantly about to fall over on top of him.[3] The story, which begins with a biblical allusion to the lamentation experienced by the Israelites at the destruction of the temple and their subsequent exile ("At the Tolstoy Museum we sat and wept.") is accompanied by several engravings, one of which, the glowering head of Tolstoy, appears on the first page and is repeated on the second with a much smaller figure of Napoleon placed in a corner, his back to the reader, contemplating the immense portrait. The reality of even Napoleon thus shrinks in comparison to Tolstoy's literary treatment of his exploits.

The same point is made in another picture of a statue-like coat around which circle tiny admirers. In still another picture, a negative of Tolstoy's monumental head is superimposed on a perspective drawing parody of the Renaissance style. Like a similar drawing of what is labeled the "Anna-Vronsky Pavilion" (showing the two lovers in a melodramatic embrace against the outlines of an open structure), the lines extend in all directions falling away finally into indefinite points outside the picture so that its subject eludes measurement. The intimidating effect of Tolstoy's presence is felt by those visitors to the museum who, transfixed by the gaze depicted in the various portraits, feel as if they have committed a small crime and have been "discovered at it by your father, who stands in four doorways, looking at you" (*CL* 45).

Unable to decide whether he agrees with those who reject this seemingly inescapable influence or those who willingly embrace it, the narrator hopes to gain inspiration from Tolstoy's work rather than his reputation despite the depression he experiences at comparing its artistry with his own. In addition to the illustrations, the story takes the form of a collection of random and chiefly trivial facts dealing with subjects such as Tolstoy's life, the construction of the museum, the reaction visitors have to its contents (among which are tiny portraits of Tolstoy's contemporaries), and even a summary of one of Tolstoy's stories, a tale whose style the narrator finds moving but distant and which teaches that everyone must worship in his own way. Toward all these, the narrator adopts an ironic and at the same time self-mocking posture that comments on the dominating influence Tolstoy's realism continues to exert on the modern consciousness. That posture, it is suggested, is the only way to bring the achievements of the past into a contemporary vision which, while startlingly different in form, somehow remains observant of it in spirit.

Artistic inspiration is also the subject of "Falling Dog," which describes the uses an artist makes of the inexplicable and accidental. At a dead end in devising new variations of his standard image—a yawning

man—the narrator, a sculptor, is literally struck by renewed possibilities for creation when a dog leaps on his
back from a third-story window. Interested primarily
in concrete form, the sculptor is cautious about transforming concept into image and tries to incorporate past
experiences and traditional art along with the experimental uses to which they might be put. "Sometimes,"
he thinks, "an image is not an image at all but merely
an idea. People have wasted years" (*CL* 35).

Nonetheless he summons every association he can
in playing with the possibilities of form as well as those
of the materials—cloth, styrofoam, plywood—out of
which he hopes to fashion a a new and vital art object.
Equally significant about his encounter is the absence
of any rational way to account for it, and accepting that
fact the sculptor embraces the dog and rushes off to his
studio to begin work. Like the form of the story itself,
which explores linguistic play without regard to meaning or to formal development, the artist views with pleasure both the process and the result. Ultimately he
accepts with gratitude the accidents that lead to aesthetic transformation and that hint at the inventive excitement still possible from surprising encounters with
familiar things.

In "The Glass Mountain," those possibilities are
frustrated by the artist's disappointment with the non-
specific but nonetheless concrete terms of city life,
among whose perils are prominently placed the difficulties of writing about it. The story takes the form of a

laborious attempt to scale a mountain which like an office building towers over the corner of Thirteenth Street and Eighth Avenue. The specificity of the location offers a comic contrast with the vague idealism that prompts the central action and is reinforced by the form the story takes. In place of organic development—events which reflect the motives of the characters and which in turn determine what happens next—each of the 100 sentences is numbered to reflect an arbitrary principle of inclusion.

At the top of the mountain, the narrator hopes to reach an enchanted symbol. The building with its "sparkling blue-white depths" is, of course, itself a symbol, as is the attempt to climb it. Like the typical mythic hero, the narrator expects to find a princess who he can free from the spell which prevents her from being recognized. The meaning of both his quest and its object, however, even of his intention, remains unclear, and though the narrator concludes that symbols are needed even by "today's stronger egos," he resolves on reaching the princess to disenchant her, an act which translates into interpreting and so limiting the layers of meaning by which she is surrounded. In the words of one of several contradictory quotations he cites, each from a different source and all ironically incongruous in context, the narrator remains committed to a "libidinous interest in reality" (*CL* 62).

Adopting a literal-minded narrative style that both reflects the structure of the story and ignores the previ-

ous failures of a host of knights, whose names he duti-
fully catalogs, the narrator comments with interest on
the manners and feel of urban life, limited chiefly to
street people with "disturbed eyes" engaged in drug
use, vandalism, and looting. Though the narrator invites the reader to witness the scene directly, the "sidewalks full of dogshit" he points to appear to him in the
brilliant colors of an artist's palette.

The central mythic pattern of the story and the
mock-dramatic heightening of the difficulties the narrator must overcome contrast with such prosaic details as
the plumber's plunger he uses in his climb, the crude
comments of his acquaintances who wait below, and
the simplistic manner of the narration itself with its extended catalogs, platitudes of literary and popular wisdom, and blow-by-blow accounts of his progress. The
narrator calls attention to this opposition by quoting
from a conventional handbook of literary terms which
distinguishes the emotionally evocative symbol of a
nightingale from the iconically limited sign, illustrated
by a traffic light, that merely signals or indicates an
object or is symptomatic of its condition. In the next
moment, he witnesses the literal combination of these
opposing terms: nightingales fly past him with traffic
lights tied to their legs.

Though it stands as the central animating principle
of the narrative, this literalization, which both blurs and
concretizes the romantic image, proves finally unsatisfying. When the narrator finally succeeds in reaching

the princess, his achievement transforms her into disappointingly limited beauty, satisfying only to the coarse demands of the crowd below to whom he promptly abandons her with disgust. Marked by ambivalence, Barthelme's comment on contemporary art and the situation of the artist appears to suggest that satisfaction with the reaches of imagination is possible only by accepting the implausible wonder of reality itself, and in the form of an eagle whose terror matches his own, the narrator cuts himself loose from that reality at the risk of missing the brilliance of the ground on which he falls.

The transformation of a romantic symbol into a more ordinary condition is precisely what faces the Phantom in "The Phantom of the Opera's Friend." Gaston Leroux's legendary figure is urged to submit to an operation which will correct his disfigurement and so allow him to resume a normal life. The focus of the story, seemingly, is on the narrator, who alternates between a melodramatic intensity of his own and a more prosaic ambition to have a normal relationship with a friend, one with whom he could travel abroad or exchange visits at their respective country estates. "A home, even marriage and children were not out of the question," he promises the Phantom (CL, 99). Sensible of the appeal held out by such a life, the Phantom nonetheless takes pleasure in his unique status. *Between three and four thousand human languages!"* he exults, *"And I am the Phantom of the Opera in every one of them!"* (CL 100). As a result, he alternately prowls the city at night

and retreats to the cellars of the Opera, where his sump-
tuous style of living rivals that of its directors but from
where his organ music continues to rise as "a communication of a kind" (*CL* 98).

Along with the grandiose and melancholic mood
swings of the Phantom, the friend's aristocratic vision
of an ordinary existence comically undercuts its promise
of a commonplace reality and, as in "The Glass Mountain," hints at a correspondingly unhappy conclusion.
When, at length, the Phantom agrees to the proposal
to surrender the mystery in which he has always envel-
oped himself, the details are arranged with a doctor
who, the friend notices, punctuates the promise of a
surgical miracle with a gesture that "extends, into the
neutral space between us, a shining scalpel" (*CL 102*).
The observation is at once chilling and suggestive. The
neutral space, particularly, seems resonant with that
transformational faculty by which, for Hawthorne, fiction was able to mediate between the actual and the
imaginary. Yet it cannot disentangle itself from the
mock importance with which Barthelme invests the
story by exploring the motivation of a flat character obsessed no longer even with his fictive purpose but with
the determination to alter the destiny given him by the
author. Barthelme's technique of unfinished sentences
suggests both dramatic urgency and the superfluousness of the completed thought. Even the original
author, Leroux is reported to have tired of his master-
piece and set it aside in order to begin some little-known

hack work. Classic and undistinguished art alike, then, spring from the same impulse and find their inspiration in the materials grounded in the popular imagination.

The peripheral or marginal expressions of popular culture clash in "Paraguay" with the vision of a utopian society shaped in large measure both by and as an expression of its language. Taken in part from a book about Tibet to which are added elements of Corbusier's design for a radiant city, the story takes the form of an everyday travelog divided into sections of disparate material organized under brief headings rather than perceived by a developing consciousnes. Barthelme's Paraguay, the narrator and travel guide acknowledges, is not the country that exists on conventional maps of South America but a new one whose existence its citizens believe is "predictive." The reference seems directed more toward art than politics and, in particular, toward a stripped-down, compressed language, whose art forms, like its sexual activity, consist solely of rules. Like new artists who, as though a scarce commodity, are "obtained" by the society, its art submits itself to the processes of industrial production and distribution. Both traditional as well as contemporary art forms are parodied. Using a mixture of computer programming and communications technology jargon, the narrator comments on the importance in Paraguay of the "hand of the artist" while describing the process of minimalization to which art, along with everything else in the country, is subjected.

THE VERNACULAR ISLES

Barthelme's parody comes closest to home, per-haps, in describing that comedy which is constructed out of a "pastiche of the emotions" "Each citizen," the reader is told, "is given as much art as his system can tolerate" (*CL* 23). Though characterized as relational, the layout of Paraguay's cities is based on the arrange-ment, along the absence of a grid, of small collections of seemingly incongruous groupings of animals—some real, some invented. The layout is another in the many acknowledgments of missing elements in Barthelme's fiction which nonetheless contribute to a substantial presence. Clothing, customs, even natural forces, all seem subject to the same arbitrary arrangements. Above all, though the narrator insists that there are no anoma-lies, no value placed on explanations which, Paraguay-ans are convinced, only bring understanding to a stop. "We try to keep everything open," one of the citizens explains, "go forward avoiding the final explanation" (*CL* 25).

Crucial to the working of the city then, and by im-plication, to the working of the story with which it is identified, is the avoidance of closure. To maintain that openness, the citizens adopt a strategy of what they describe as "creative misunderstanding." The strategy does not dispel anxieties and, in fact, is responsible for the creation of new ones. Such anxieties, however, are at least playfully reconstituted in new categories. Noth-ing in the country remains fixed. Behavior patterns are random, governed solely, the reader is comically advised, by the Brownian movement of atomic particles. Not only the rate but the nature of activity is affected by changes in temperature and even the architecture is constantly in motion. Concrete walls are divided into doors of differing heights, colors, and thicknesses whose configurations are made to be continually changing. Motion is also a function of unusual combinations by means of which language creates new realities. Boquets are seen to open like umbrellas, rain falls in heavy yellow drops like pancake batter. The menace of ocean waves to prospective bathers is measured in carefully calibrated degrees. Abstract issues are fused into a "skelp" of questions and answers before being passed through a series of caresses.

The contradictions that emerge from this fusion of surprising elements are reflected in the plan of the city which is kept in a locked box to which everyone has a key and which is designed to allow "a very wide range of tendencies to interact." It is this democratic principle on which Barthelme's fiction also operates; yet the equality of all objects carries its own penalties. The smoothness with which affairs are conducted translates itself into the physical properties of Paraguay, where citizens experience a problem with shedding skin, and even the sand is sifted twice a day to remove impurities and maintain its whiteness. Another aspect of the striving for purity is the widespread use of microminiaturization which results in everything in Paraguay getting smaller and smaller and "leaves enormous spaces to be

THE VERNACULAR ISLES

filled." Echoing the self-parody Barthelme introduces in the "minimized" statements of the country's art, these spaces cause men to wander about them "trying to touch something." Finally when, like the startling word combinations, the narrator is chosen for a ceremonial role on the principle of the "least-likely leader," it is uncertain whether his attempt to establish order results in his entering or leaving the country.

The wide range of tendencies which continue to interact in the story thus serve as a paradigm for the method Barthelme employs to write it. Much like the country's red snow, it glows with an inner illumination and is walled off from the population yet not forbidden to them. The reader, like the citizens of Paraguay, is accordingly left with an "ongoing low-grade mystery," one that invites contemplation but that "there was no point in solving" (CL 27).

The blankness ironically presented in Paraguay in the potentially dreary expanse of concrete wall is graphically demonstrated in "The Explanation" by black squares, which testify to the enduring quality of things despite their problematic relations or, more accurately, the absence of such relations, while, like the black paintings of Ad Reinhardt, they additionally suggest a sharp break with the practices of the past. The squares conceal a machine about which elliptical conversations are conducted by two voices designated only as Q and A. Such exchanges subsequently reappear in several of Barthelme's stories, often pitting an aggressive, probing questioner against a hesitant respondent. Typically they begin with no reference to what has preceded them, jump abruptly to, alternate with, or repeat observations (often about sex) or trail off in parenthetical summaries which suggest that even the author has become impatient with the digressive style. The questions and answers explain nothing and ultimately lead to a reversal of the positions initially held by the antagonists. Though Q, for example, begins by challenging A to define the machine, he is himself finally maneuvered into an interpretation of it that is obscured by philosophical jargon, unaccountably gives way to a photograph of his daughter, and finally leads to the admission that "reasons and conclusions exist although they exist elsewhere, not here" (CL 78).

Bewildered by the machine which Q struggles to describe in terms of human features, A is more concerned with his imagined social inadequacy and with erotic fantasies to which it presumably gives rise. Q proves equally interested in those fantasies which lead to his admission that he is bored by the machine, which he nonetheless tries to persuade his mistrustful companion is superior to art. His critique takes the form of computer jargon whose list-like "error messages" mirror the disconnected nature of the conversation itself.

Q's description of the machine's function proves equally applicable to that of fiction and, in particular, to the informing principle of the story. "We construct these machines [he claims] not because we confidently expect them to do what they are designed to do—change the government in this instance—but because we intuit a machine out there, glowing like a shopping center" (*CL* 72). Q thus transforms the nature of art into an object that rejects not only didactic intent but even authorial origin and that, while determining its own form, draws its energy from the commonplace commercial elements of the environment. It is this last quality, perhaps, which leads him to assert the "bravery" of machines and A to the somewhat ambivalent echo that "machines are braver than art" (*CL* 77).

Bored with artistic no less than mechanical concerns—the novel as an art form is dead he admits, and his nose bleeds at even the mention of further reading—A approves of Q's jumbled computer messages and subsequently is instructed in a catechism touching on art, mathematics, and political philosophy that arrives at the irrational as an alternative to reasoned rhetoric. Predictably, the logic proves circular; madness is found to be the consequence of the attempt to inject purity into rhetoric. Language as a reference of reality thus becomes the object of the ironic exchange which ends with a comic reference to rhetoric as a tool of political manipulation. Even the question-and-answer form is subject to ironic self-examination. In contrast to Q's professed belief in its value, A expresses only qualified approval: "I am bored with it [he admits] but I realize it

UNDERSTANDING DONALD BARTHELME

permits many valuable omissions: what kind of day it is, what I'm wearing, and what I'm thinking. That's a very considerable advantage, I would say" (*CL* 73).

Though the nature of the advantage remains unstated, the disappearance of conventional signs of physical actuality or of social or psychological attributes that constitute a fixed identity allows the reader to confront language directly rather than approach reality through the transparent forms of fiction. Such absences, which in fact constitute the informing principle of the conversation, are reinforced by a series of grammatically simply statements which display little continuity and resemble nothing so much as the exercises in translation of an introductory text for the study of a foreign language. The nonsensical, often-repeated statements— "The chair is here." "I spoke to a tourist." "I knocked at the door." "We shall not cross the river."—which alternate with other subjects—art, science, erotic fantasy—provide a gloss on the difficulties of the story. Like the explanations Q identifies as not real in the sense that they are not touchable, the problem presented by fiction rests in the attempt to see it as an equivalent or translation of reality. A acknowledges his difficulty in telling one object from another; books, trees, sentences, all seem alike to him. Only films or images are distinctive, and though, revealingly, he dislikes having his own picture taken and expresses only perfunctory interest in a picture of Q's daughter, he persists in dreaming about a former lover long after she has married someone else.

What finally defines A's posture and subjects it to the concluding irony of the story is an interest in purity and in the exceptional, to which he alludes in what appears to be a digression that Q shrewdly recognizes as a confession. For his part, Q converts the terms of A's erotic fantasies into abstract equivalents for operating the machine. Only by reducing experience to a single plane, he concludes, can "the mutual good of all categories" be realized, and though unable to complete his thought Q searches in the phenomena of the masses for the possibility of exceptional and rare events.

The same themes are addressed in "Kierkegaard Unfair to Schlegel," a companion story to "The Explanation" that has deservedly received much wider recognition. Once again Q and A are locked in debate which is constantly interrupted by, but takes no notice of, the sexual fantasy A relates. Though the exchange takes on something of the quality of a therapy session, Q insists that he is not A's doctor. The ostensible subjects once again are politics, the opposition of humanistic and technological aspects of culture, and the generally desperate and indistinguishable means by which society tries to keep itself amused. What emerges from this discussion is A's defence of the ironic responses he makes in order to distance himself from the boredom he identifies in this meaningless activity. To do so he launches into a subtle examination of Kierkegaard's *The Concept of Irony*, which, he points out, argues that irony negatively frees the ironist from the world by depriving the object of its reality. Using Kierkegaard's attack on Schlegel's romantic novel *Lucinde* as a case in point, A summarizes the argument that poetry attempts to achieve a higher actuality than that afforded by the imperfections of history and so alleviates its misery. A quotes Kierkegaard's objection that "what is wanted . . . is not a victory over the world but a reconciliation with the world" (*CL* 89). Such a reconciliation, Kierkegaard insists, can be provided only by religion. Though A rejects this argument, in part because, he claims, it does not view Schlegel's work itself as an object, he inserts a black box similar to those in "The Explanation" after which he dismisses his previous explanation. The real reason for his quarrel, A admits, is Kierkegaard's implied criticism of his own ironic posture, and though A claims to love this irony, he haltingly acknowledges that it affords only a poor, unsatisfactory pleasure.

Earlier, A proposed that the semifashionable practice of wearing surplus army uniforms created an imitation or clown army that erased the difference between the real and the invented. Rather than distancing itself from ordinary reality, such clowning in the story moves similarly to close the gap between it and imagination. The same function is underscored in a series of questions Q asks one after another without waiting for answers. "How is my car?" Q wants to know. "How is my button?" "How is my mad mother?" "How is the aphorism I left with you?" The questions prohibit response by failing to specify the quality which is their unstated subject or provide a context in which they might make sense. "How tight did you sew my button?" Q might have demanded. "How comfortable is my mad mother?" "How pertinent is the aphorism I left with you?" Interpretation, in short, becomes impossible. The frustration A experiences with this condition subsequently leads to the following exchange in which A is made to surrender his irony:

A: These imbecile questions . . .
Q: Inadequately answered. . . .
A: . . . imbecile questions leading nowhere . . .
Q: The personal abuse continues.
A:..that voice, confident and shrill . . .
Q: (aside): He has given away his gaiety, and now has nothing (*CL* 93).

Well, not quite nothing. When Q relates a moving anecdote about Pasteur, A responds bitterly and with an echo of his former irony, "Yes, that makes up for everything, that you know that story. . . ." (*CL* 93). Modernist irony which expressed a sense of alienation has thus, as Allen Wilde has convincingly demonstrated, shifted from a technique of satire to an autonomous vision, depicting "the figure of the outsider, the uncommited spectator, longing to overcome his self-consciousness

UNDERSTANDING DONALD BARTHELME

and make contact with the world outside his limited and limiting ego"[4] What is equally significant about Barthelme's story is not the content of its argument but the joking manner which shows that the argument cannot be resolved one way or the other in part because both positions remove discourse from the world and so blend indistinguishably into each other.

A more practical if still not altogether satisfactory solution to this dilemma is propsed in the title story, "City Life," where the modern problem as stated by one of the characters "is not angst but a lack of angst" (*CL* 165). In this environment, the struggle of art is simply to remain necessary. It also proves to be the struggle that marks the characters' lives. The story traces in 21 numbered segments the arrival in the city of two law students, Ramona and Elsa, who become roommates and rivals in both their careers and in their personal relationships. Excluded by the sexual current set up between Elsa and her lover Charles, Ramona goes through the motions of housekeeping while scheming to become part of the energy she senses around her. After several affairs, none of which proves finally satisfying, she arranges to kidnap Charles. Ramona's plan, though successful, ends inconclusively. Charles becomes one of three men whose names she continues to juggle in arbitrary patterns that, as Elsa points out, suggest "she has been engaging in hilarity at the expense of the law" (*CL* 155).

Elsa becomes involved with a young revolutionary

named Jacques, whose degrees were earned at the New Yorker Theatre, where, he recalls the "glorious debris" underneath the seats and the movies whose unreality are symbolized for him by the laughing aristocrats who are often their subjects. The combination of the debris and the romantic anachronism of the aristocrats (they are pictured as arriving in phaetons and tumbrels from places as various as Flushing and Sao Paulo) not only describes the city, it is echoed in the revolutionary form Barthelme employs in writing the story. Though Charles believes himself imprisoned in the aristocratic tradition which, when threatened, is representatively pictured by the enraged aristocrats whose raised canes "shattered in the sun, like a load of antihistamines falling out of an airplane," his vision of them similarly reflects a contemporary awareness. He imagines:

Laughing aristocrats who invented the cost-plus contract . . . Laughing aristocrats who invented the real estate broker . . . Laughing aristocrats who invented Formica . . . (*CL* 158).

In Heineken beer, whose green brilliance evokes the colorful possibilities of the commonplace, Charles toasts "To the struggle!" and implicit in that ambivalent challenge, for which no political referent is given, is the one Barthelme has undertaken to liberate fiction from the constricting form of tradition.

The terms in which that struggle will be conducted

are further suggested by the performance of a folk ritual whose purpose Ramona questions. "Is that supposed to make the sun shine, or what?" she demands and is told, "Oh, I think it's just sort of to . . . honor the sun. I don't think it's supposed to make it do anything" (*CL* 156). That principle is affirmed by Charles for whom not only the content but even the processes of art are aleatoric, subject to chance and so problematic. Faced with an empty canvas and the difficulty of remaining within the tradition while bringing to it an individualizing perspective, the painter, Charles explains, can begin by making an arbitrary mark just in order to have something on the canvas:

Then he is profoundly depressed because what is there is not what he meant. And it's time for lunch. He goes out and buys a pastrami sandwich meanwhile regarding the canvas with the wrong mark on it out of the corner of his eye. During the afternoon, he paints out the mark of the morning. This affords him a measure of satisfaction. The balance of the afternoon is spent in deciding whether or not to venture another mark. The new mark, if one is ventured, will also, inevitably, be misconceived. He ventures it. It is misconceived. It is, in fact, the worst kind of vulgarity. He paints out the second mark. Anxiety accumulates. However, the canvas is now, in and of itself, because of the wrong moves and the painting out, becoming rather interesting looking . . . The canvas is, for one thing, no longer empty . . . A something has been wrested from the nothing (*CL* 157–58).

As a coda to this summary, Charles points out that the quality of the object remains in question and that, in fact, the whole artistic enterprise may be dated by changes in the nature of the way art is conceived. Charles's thought, like the art he describes, appropriately remains incomplete. Additionally, he has difficulty establishing a link between that description and the conversation (and by implication the artistic motives) which prompted it. Nonetheless he does locate within the tormented and tentative processes of art a presence and an immediacy that marks as chiefly irrelevant the esoteric issues raised in connection with them.

These concerns are advanced by the housepainters Emmanuel and Curtis, who can paint and watch movies on TV at the same time and whose commerical profession casts an ironic light on the cultural pretentions of high art. Their casual indifference to the colors they are called upon to use serves as a paradigm of the need in Barthelme's fiction to look for coherence outside the internal logic established by the interaction of character with situation. That interaction emerges in the movie titles Ramona and Elsa find listed in a newspaper which share a common term but which feature constantly shifting casts. The same principle accounts for the lyrics and chord progression of the popular songwriter Moonbelly, one of Ramona's lovers, whose hit record, "The System Cannot Withstand Close Scrutiny," is introduced at a concert for younger people and, like "Views of My Father Weeping," ends with "etc." Moonbelly nonetheless concludes that "Cities are erotic," but qualifies that judgment by adding "in a depressing way" (*CL* 164).

Viewing the law as another way at which Barthelme gets at the problem of art and society illuminates the exchange between the two women when Elsa becomes pregnant and decides to give up law school. "The law needs knowledgeable civilians as well as practitioners," Ramona consoles her, establishing criteria for readers as well as writers, "Your training will not be wasted" (*CL* 157). Ramona takes the idea of training or artistic professionalism to the opposite extreme. Rejecting the sexual invitation of the city announced in Moonbelly's bestselling song "Cities Are Centers of Copulation," Ramona can conceive of creativity solely in terms of the miraculous. She convinces herself that she has been made pregnant by the glances of the people around her:

From the millions of units crawling about on the surface of the city, their wavering desirous eye selected me. The pupil enlarged to admit more light: more me. They began dancing little dances of suggestion and fear. These dances constitute an invitation of unmistakable import—an invitation which, if accepted, leads one down many muddy roads. I accepted. What was the alternative? (*CL* 167–68).

Often taken by critics as an affirmation of the possibilities open to her, the acceptance is highly qualified, an expression of helpless submission rather than enthusiastic choice. Ramona's unhappiness with her options is underscored by her description of the city to which they uniformly lead:

I have to admit [she thinks] we are locked in the most exquisite mysterious muck. This muck heaves and palpitates. It is multi-directional and has a mayor. To describe it takes many hundreds of thousand of words. Our muck is only a part of a much greater muck—the nation-state—which is itself the creation of that muck of mucks, human consciousness (*CL* 166–67).

The sense of confinement evoked by the verb "locked" and by the unpleasantly yielding associations generated by muck are reinforced by the heaving, pulsating motion of the city which suggests the unnatural animation of an organ in some horror movie, artifically kept alive in a jellied solution by an electrical device. Civic government is, in fact, linked with a quality ("it is multidirectional") usually attributed to objects that measure distances or register electrical signals, such as a rangefinder or an antenna. Yet the picture is not all bleak. Despite the hundred of thousands of words it takes to describe city life, perhaps only by means of them, a measure of sublimity and mystery, Ramona is convinced, attaches to it, especially when Moonbelly sings or when all the lights go out.

Ramona's restlessness, signaled by the arrangement and rearrangement of names by which she attempts to order her relationships, has earlier been brought into relief by the arrival of Elsa's parents from Montana. Her mother, overly solicitous, her father, apprehensive about having his car stolen, explode the stereotype of regional parochialism by bringing as a housewarming gift an original print by Rene Magritte. When Elsa wonders where to hang it, she is advised succinctly, "How about on the wall?" For Ramona, walls, like most other things in her life, do not have such reassuring solidity. After viewing a movie in which a native community is menaced by a man-eating tiger, she speculates on the threats faced by modern city dwellers, among which she places prominently the high cost of electricity. As in her pregnancy, she can only imagine a collective civic response, hypothetical rather than actual, in which New Yorkers telepathically agree to resist by refusing to pay their bills. "The same thought," she fantasizes, "drifts across the furrowed surface of nine million minds. We wink at each other, through the walls" (*CL* 167). The shared thought, the sense of complicity, the surface it plays across, the figures invited to share in the urban dance of fear and suggestion, are all made transparent through the walls of Ramona's fiction. On one side of them, these ghostly figures acknowledge with a comic wink their protest. On the other, Barthelme and the reader stand winking back.

Notes

1. "Hiding Man," *Come Back, Dr. Caligari* (New York: Little, Brown, 1967) 33.

2. See Jerome Klinkowitz, "Donald Barthelme," in *The New Fiction: Interviews with Innovative American Writers*, ed. Joe David Bellamy (Urbana: University of Illinois Press, 1974), 53–54. At the end of this interview, Barthelme invents a parodically exaggerated news story purporting to recant his faith in fragments as an aesthetic principle.

3. Jochen Achilles, "Donald Barthelme's Aesthetic of Inversion: Caligari's Come-Back as Caligari's Leave-Taking," *The Journal of Narrative Technique* 12 (Spring 1982); 109–10.

4. Alan Wilde, *Horizons of Assent: Modernism, Postmodernism, and the Ironic Imagination* (Baltimore: Johns Hopkins UP, 1981) 178.

CHAPTER THREE

Barthelme the Scrivener

Art, Barthelme insists, cannot *not* think of the world.[1] Accordingly, in his fiction, the function of art and the situation of the artist provides an enabling metaphor by which it becomes possible to come to terms with a resistant and often opaque reality, whose disappointment and confusions are not so much dispelled by language as mediated, or, in the best case, perhaps even confronted by it in such a way as to change, if not the world, then at least the reader's awareness of its possibilities. The stories about art seldom interrogate either its meanings or its effect, other than on the artists themselves and the difficulties they experience in creating it. As an object in the fictive landscape, then, art as art, like the urban settings or the figures that inhabit them in much of Barthelme's fiction, emerges more in outline than in any realized depth.

Calling attention to the situation of Barthelme's artistic narrators, Wayne Stengel points to their insistence on a more meaningful reality than one provided by the art itself. At the same time, Stengel notes, they "regard art as a self-contained object without necessary meaning beyond its surface appearance or assumed reference to a world outside itself."[2] The lack of a recognizable environment does not, as Stengel argues that it does, ask the reader to become involved in the process of the story. Rather, as part of that process, it resists interpretation in favor of reimagining ordinary reality. In "How I Write My Songs," another of the previously uncollected stories which appeared in *Sixty Stories*, the parody of the creative process revolves around the simplistic explanations the narrator provides of his method and the naïvete of his imitative approach. Despite the copybook account which reduces the art of songwriting to a commercial formula, despite the misspellings ("When I lost my baby/I almost lost my mine") which suggest the writer has little understanding of the sense and no authentic idea of the feeling behind his traditional lyrics, despite the clichéd sentiment with which he concludes, the elemental force of the lyrics confirms the narrator's conviction that "what may appear to be rather plain or dull on paper becomes quite different when it is a song."[3]

The blankness or opacity, the discontinuities, interruptions, digressions, hesitations, incompleted thoughts, elliptical structure, and uncertain reference of language, all subject the narrative to a compression that both invests it with an intensity and places it seemingly beyond the reach of thematic focus. Just such a focus is given, however, by a comic perspective that, in

American fiction at least, reaches back to the nineteenth century example of Herman Melville's "Bartleby the Scrivener." Built around the metaphor of a writer and the public, Melville's elusive parable describes the conflict between an eccentric law copyist and his seemingly obtuse employer. The specific circumstances of the tale are left pretty much untold. Almost childlike, even petulant in his stony refusal to accept either instruction or request, Bartleby offers nothing to account for his behavior. About his past, the lawyer admits, "nothing is ascertainable except from original sources, and in his case, those are very small."[4] In fact, original sources prove inaccessible. This lack of origins does not serve as the animating force of the story by prompting Bartleby to go in search of them. Rather it is a condition deliberately imposed by the scrivener, who will tell the lawyer nothing about himself or even indicate any reasonable objections he might have to such disclosure.

Bartleby's negation, in fact, appears so comprehensive as to convert his protest against meaninglessness into a statement of it. Indifferent as an inanimate object to any claims upon him, Bartleby is, at the same time, immovable as any natural force. His refusal of every suggestion the lawyer makes about employment while continuing to insist that he is not particular (a term which in context thus has significant resonance) suggests the joke with which the appeals for reason are uniformly greeted throughout Melville's fiction. In ironic counterpoint to the bust of Cicero at which he

BARTHELME THE SCRIVENER

stares and mirroring its vacant, eyeless sockets, Bartleby's eloquent silence is, in fact, universal. His ultimately infectious habit of using the term "prefer" gives the illusion of choice to what proves an insistent if not immiscible condition. His opposition to fate, then, becomes itself the judgment of fate—equally cold and inflexible, ubiquitous, finally imprisoning no less than silently imprisoned. Bartleby, in short, changes from a victim of an indifferent universe to a symbol of its negation.

As with so much else in this puzzling tale, Melville leaves uncertain the lawyer's relation to his clerk; yet this, too, becomes somewhat less intimidating when it is seen in the context of a joke. If Bartleby is unwilling to perform the functions of a scrivener, the lawyer, a self-acknowledged storyteller takes delight in the sound of words and is able to find an element of beauty even in the blankness of walls. Neither in his legal nor his literary manner does the lawyer evidence any interest in originality. He describes himself as a "conveyancer and title hunter" and, in fact, becomes himself a copyist, not only imitating even the characteristic expression Bartleby employs but also echoing for a time the scrivener's withdrawal into self-imposed isolation. In an effort to elude those who, like the landlord of his former offices or the current tenants who persist in holding him accountable for Bartleby's continued occupancy, he reduces his lifestyle to a minimum, consisting chiefly of fugitive visits to the suburbs and, in what can only be the last stages of desperation, to Jersey City and Hoboken.

Despite his smug boast of safety, then, a boast which, it turns out, is mistaken, his pride in his prudence and method, above all, his overblown rhetoric, the lawyer is able, as Bartleby is not, to displace a "doctrine of assumptions" with an awareness of the "noise and heat and joy of the roaring thoroughfares at noon" (128). It is, in fact, precisely this intermingling of classical and commonplace, the punctuation of exaggerated narrative formality with sly hints of self-awareness, deliberately concealed backgrounds, and abruptly transformed characters, that caution against too great a preoccupation with interpreting life and a consequent loss of its more substantial immediacy, even within the framework of literary construction, perhaps within that framework most of all. The resistance of rhetoric to interpretation allows the lawyer elegiacally to commiserate not only with humanity but even with the principle of emptiness that opposes it.[5] Recognizing the inescapability of that confrontation, the lawyer shows as well the tragi-comic possibilities with which, as scrivener, he can mediate with reality. And in telling the story, he settles for a rueful acceptance of the fact that there is no way to make sense of it and that no answers, now or in future, will be forthcoming.

For Barthelme, as for Melville, these limited possibilities remain centered in the object of representation and, in particular, in its distinctive verbal quality rather

BARTHELME THE SCRIVENER

than in the formal unity of its disparate elements, perhaps most prominent among them, the unnamed but
isolating horror and the "domestic associations" without whose humanizing influence, the lawyer is convinced, one is led even to acts of murder, or, more
poignantly, in whose absence the indifferent scrivener
is seen to waste away. *Sadness*, Barthelme's fourth collection of short stories, seems to mark a shift in emphasis in his work that recognizes in the presence of the
commonplace a necessary balance to the nihilistic
horrors accompanied in such earlier stories as "The Policeman's Ball" (*City Life*) by a hooting chorus of melodramatic laughter. And while maintaining their emotional detachment, the stories additionally seem to find
the dilemmas of modern existence less a subject for bemused indifference, or even playful hilarity, than for
tense recognition and for exploration of the often parallel difficulties faced by the artist. The sadness of the
title, accordingly, refers to the largely domestic anxieties prompted by the exaggerated expectations generated in literary forms and the consequent inability to
satisfy those expectations. Such disappointment leads
to the separation of the couple in "Critique de la Vie
Quotidienne," which, Barthelme has acknowledged,
was salvaged from an earlier attempt at a novel.[6] The
narrator and his wife, Wanda, struggle unsuccessfully
to cope with the banalities of everyday life and, in particular, with the demands of child-rearing. The results
are discouraging. "The world in the evening seems

fraught with the absence of promise," the narrator complains, "if you are a married man."[7] The qualification which opposes evening and romance to the daily routine of marriage is crucial and points to an unwillingness to deal with limits. The consequence of such childish self-absorption (the wife sucks her thumb while the narrator yells at their child; he retreats from the marriage in alcoholism and hostility), is envy of the extravagant displays of wealth in their society, mutual antagonism, and a general state of boredom. When the couple is confronted with the limits of mortality by death-masks their child has learned to make at school, the father demands to know the meaning of the knowing look with which the child displays them. "You'll find out," he is warned. The refusal to heed that warning leads to a divorce, whose appearance of civility breaks down into mutual recrimination and an attempt by the wife to shoot her ex-husband. Not even this dramatic expression of buried feeling marks a change in their lives. Following the divorce, Wanda immerses herself in the study of esoteric subjects, the narrator attempts to soothe his own fear of death with the anticipation of a limitless supply of scotch whiskey, and the child is placed, significantly, in an experimental nursery.

The same exhaustion, preoccupation with the trivial, and self-absorption in contemporary culture informs "The Party," which begins with the admission by the narrator that "I went to a party and corrected a pronounciation" (*S* 57). Unable to distinguish between significant variations of art and influenced by movie cliché expressions of anxiety ("Drums, drums, drums, outside the windows"), the guests are indifferent even to the arrival at the party of the sudden towering figure of King Kong ("Giant hands, black, thick with fur, reaching in through the windows" (*S* 57), a pop-culture icon of brute passion combined with sentimentality. Kong's menace, it turns out, has been acculturated; the ape now teaches art history at a public university, where his interest is in seduction rather than primitive expression of desire.

Like the others in the room, the narrator remains largely passive and pessimistic about his chances to break out of the torpor which envelops his generation with its "emphasis on emotional cost control as well as its insistent, almost annoying lucidity." The annoyance stems from the refusal to confront the problems inherent in ordinary life. "What made us think," the narrator asks rhetorically, "that we would escape things like bankruptcy, alcoholism, being disappointed, having children?" (*S* 62). Though uncomfortable in this environment, in which ambitious people desperate for entertainment reduce experience to word games and in which literary fashion substitutes for felt response ("Now that you have joined us in finding Kafka, and Kleist, too, the awesome figures that we have agreed that they are"), he can only appeal to his companion, Francesca, to take some decisive action which will enable them to leave (*S* 62). Her refusal to leave the party does not indicate contentment with her situation or even a fundamental difference with the narrator's philosophy. In a kind of helpless self-justification that is often exchanged by a couple regretfully agreeing to the necessity of a divorce, he insists, "Of course we did everything right, insofar as we were able to imagine what 'right' was" (*S* 62). In the social climate that continues to make extravagant demands for fulfillment, such efforts prove resistant even to the compelling power of words. "When one has spoken a lot," the narrator is persuaded, "one has already used up all of the ideas one has. You must change the people you are speaking to so that you appear, to yourself, to be still alive" (*S* 61).

Change mistaken for the appearance of vitality also marks the manner in which the narrator attempts to deal with his inability either to understand or meaningfully affect his circumstances and leads to a final appeal to Francesca to reject him so that he may try something else. In the absence of any response from her, the narrator is unable to make one of his own or even to believe any longer that discriminations of value are necessary. "Is it really important to know that this movie is fine, and that one terrible," he concludes hopelessly, "and to talk intelligently about the difference? Wonderful elegance! No good at all!" (*S* 62).

The self-doubt which leads to that final dispiriting assessment is more hopefully resolved in "The Temptation of Saint Anthony" by the assertion of value in the sheer phenomenal quality of existence. The story is narrated by one of the members of a local community in which St. Anthony takes up residence. In contrast to his neighbors for whom, he notes waspishly, "everything is hard enough without having to deal with something that is not tangible and clear" (*S* 151), and who consequently find the higher orders of abstraction to be a nuisance, the narrator claims to find them interesting. What he admires chiefly is the marvelous or ineffable which, he contends, in a world of mundanity allows the saint to shine. His sense of decency, to some extent self-congratulatory, misses the point. St. Anthony unexpectedly reveals a fondness for such banal delights as fried foods and department store carpeting and diplomatically adopts an offhand manner designed to make his presence less disturbing to the community. It is these temptations of the commonplace—the attractive quality of things—that he must struggle with. His aescetic refusal to give in to them finally prevents his ability to choose, and, toward the end of his residence in the community, he is heard to say only the word "Or."

When Camilla, an unconventional if provocative young woman of the town, accuses him of attempting some physical intimacy, this lack of definition rather than any truth to the accusation leads St. Anthony to return to the desert. But not without a final, unsettling revelation. Less an escape from the alternatives of ordinary life than an exclusion from them, the saint amus-

UNDERSTANDING DONALD BARTHELME

ingly confesses to the narrator in the last line of the story that he regarded the temptations as "entertainment."

The refusal to take the whole thing seriously hints at the attitude Barthelme encourages the reader to adopt as well. Though the narrator's response to the saint is sympathetic, his folksy tone and gossipy manner, at odds with his use of sophisticated diction, his pretentious moralizing, and his fondness for the abstract, work against his authority as an authorial surrogate. He is narrowly judgmental about Camilla who, he points out, "went to the Sorbonne and studied some kind of philosophy called 'structure' with somebody named Levy who is supposed to be very famous" (*S* 158). Overly insistent on his indifference to the possibility of the saint's having given in to sexual temptation, and seemingly unaware of the implied condescension in his boast of periodic visits to the saint when he is not vacationing with his wife in Florida, he ironically (and, for the purposes of the story, unknowingly) condemns those people who resent St. Anthony's indifference to the material world and wish he would "go out and get a job, like everybody else." Thus the narrator values St. Anthony for the very qualities of withdrawal the story works to resist. In a deeply human if ambiguous sense, he cannot accept the idea of the ordinary as itself exceptional and yet recognizes that "you have to keep the ordinary motors of life running in the meantime" (*S* 153).

BARTHELME THE SCRIVENER

In "The Sandman," the narrator reaches something of the same conclusion. "The best thing to do," he advises, "is just to do ordinary things, read the newspaper, for example, or watch basketball, or wash the dishes" (*S* 95). Sometimes taken as a defense of imagination or art, the story takes the form of a letter to Dr. Hodder, a psychiatrist, who regards the desire of his patient Susan to terminate analysis and buy a piano instead as symptomatic of her illness and so of her need to continue analysis. Normative and aberrant behavior quickly become reversed. Written by Susan's boyfriend, who, like St. Anthony, is confronted by the prospect of seemingly limitless alternatives, the letter acknowledges the hidden impulses that may account for behavior but sees in them an accurate reflection of conditions that may respond more to neglect than to treatment. "What do you do with a patient who finds the world unsatisfactory?" he asks, "The world *is* unsatisfactory; only a fool would deny it" (*S* 95). In contrast, then, to the utopian impulse to which he drily alludes in the repeated song refrain, "The world is waiting for the sunrise," the narrator insists that he is content with Susan "as is," an acceptance of the ability to affect experience, not merely the way we think about it, that is as equally distant from Ramona's reluctant acknowledgment of the world's throbbing sexuality as it is from the psychiatrist's attempt at normative manipulation.

This reductive concern for the ordinary projected in a "muted series of irritation, frustrations, and baffle-

ments" rather than in the more dramatic emotions of
existential dread has led the critic Alan Wilde to find in
Barthelme's fiction the possibilities for a more dynamic
response than that promised solely by the modernist
escape to a vision of fictive order.[8] Life in Barthelme's
fiction, Wilde concludes, has become less mysterious
but more puzzling, by which I take him to mean that it
has lost not only its belief in the supernatural but in the
ability and even the desire of fiction to convincingly
represent that belief. As a result, it preempts the struggle of characters to search for meaning within the text
and moves instead from a self-contained world which
circumscribes their existence toward an enveloping one
that accounts for their reality, in other words, moves
from the interior to the surface of a work.

That movement is facilitated by the illustrations
which, as in "At the Tolstoy Museum," once again reduce the text to the status of a caption in "The Flight of
Pigeons from the Palace." The story addresses the ever-
increasing demands of the public for sensational performance by the artist and consequently conceives of art
as a collection of sideshow exhibits at a circus or an
old-fashioned theater bill. "It is difficult to keep the public interested," the narrator explains, and lists among
the promised attractions The Prime Rate, Edgar Allan
Poe, and The Sale of the Public Library, before concluding with the announcement of a new volcano, pictured
with suitable irony in the middle of an eruption. The
illustrations include numbered drawings from an anat-

omy text, statues, groupings of figures in different styles and from different historical eras, as well as mock Renaissance-style perspective drawings which, as R. E. Johnson points out, flatten the illusion by projecting the lines which are superimposed on the central image off the drawing into some infinite point beyond where the picture can be seen to begin or end.[9] What is perhaps most significant about these illustrations, however, is the contrast between the accuracy of the descriptions and the tortured interpretations which the narrator draws from them. Literal representation, Barthelme appears to suggest, is not by itself either immune to or a refuge against the distortions of the imagination.

Art seems to consent to its own destruction in "Supoena," which indirectly addresses the framing conditions that link the narrative to the world in which it exists. The narrator is sent a tax notice from the obscurely sinister "Bureau of Compliance" on a robot or surrogate called Charles he has built to, among other things, "instruct him in complacency." Like the audience demands in "The Flight of Pigeons from the Palace," the tax seems greater than the narrator's ability to pay and forces him to disassemble the robot. The consequences remain ambivalent. Charles's detachment from social conditions and the obligation to take some action to alleviate them serve as an example for the narrator's own posture. Looking at him, the narrator confesses, "I said to myself, 'See, it is possible to live in the world and not change the world'" (*S* 116). Charles thus functions a surrogate not only for the narrator but for fiction itself. In this regard, he suggests a role which balances impersonal objectivity with the need for immersion in the everyday. "Without Charles," the narrator realizes with alarm, "without his example, his exemplary quietude, I run the risk of acting, the risk of risk. I must participate. I must leave the house and walk about" (*S* 116). Displacing to fiction his obligation to become involved in reality, the narrator not only evades that responsibility but reduces fictive possibilities as well. His desperate cry, then, is not exclusively an expression of repressed emotion or even an appeal for involvement in experience. It is a statement of the ambivalence with which fiction must address the often conflicting requirements of actuality and imagination, the opposing claims of didactic and aesthetic impulses, the demands of form and those of feeling.

The artist-hero of "Engineer-Private Paul Klee Misplaces an Aircraft between Milbertshofen and Cambrai, March 1916" provides an indication of how Barthelme hopes to reconcile those demands in his struggle with both his art and the the Secret Police. Drafted into the army, Klee has been assigned to escort a train transporting aircraft to various bases across Germany but takes more interest in the life around him. His interior monologues alternate with those of the police, who watch closely to discover what he is doing and learn, as they reveal, his secret, really the secret of his art. This proves to be Klee's concern with the ordinary course of his life: the sale of his drawings, the meaninglessness of the war, the arrangements he makes to meet his lover. In a statement that echoes the process of art described in "City Life," he points out, "There are always unexpected delays, reroutings, backtrackings" (S 65), but while concentrating on its details—"He is reading a book of Chinese short stories." "He has removed his boots. His feet rest twenty-six centimeters from the baggage-car stove."—the police are unable to see their significance (S 66). Klee is more concerned with the quality of experience. "These Chinese short stories are slight and lovely," he thinks (S 66). When he notices one of the planes unaccountably missing, he decides to alter the manifest (the artist, he observes, is not so different from the forger) and to replace the plane with a drawing. The drawing, however, is not of the plane but of its absence, and it is this absence-as-presence which allows the police to accept, if not fully appreciate, the contradictions they have attempted to monitor. The association of the police with critics is suggested in their final assessment of Klee's achievement:

We would like to embrace him as a comrade and brother but unfortunately we are not embraceable. We are secret, we exist in the shadows, the pleasure of the comradely/brotherly embrace is one of the pleasures we are denied, in our dismal service (S 70).

But if criticism is short, art, Klee is aware, like chocolate, meltingly sweet, at once temporary and eternal, goes on forever.

In "The Catechist," art out of the machine emerges in the confession of a 40-year-old priest who has fallen in love with a married woman and who responds to the incantatory and comic catalog of the way hatred of Sundays is expressed in various countries with a contrasting specificity of detail. The strategy of naming and, in particular, of naming absences thus serves as a means not only of calling them into being but of acknowledging their magical existence. It is this existence in all its variousness which prompted the priest's sense of vocation. Asked by the catechist if he initially heard a call, he replies "I heard many things. Screams. Suites for unaccompanied cello" (*S* 125).

In contrast to a postage-sized Old Testament the catechist produces and almost at once replaces in favor of a button on which is printed the word "Love," the priest remembers the picture on a stamp he used to mail a letter to his lover and responds to his superior's dry textbook formula for dealing with apathy with the following recognition: "I think: Analysis terminable and interminable. I think: Then she will leave the park looking backward over her shoulder" (*S* 125). As opposed to the interpretation, it is the perceived instant that stirs the emotion (of the catechist as well as the sinful priest) so that what endures, paradoxically, is the perishable human gesture, whose meaning rests entirely in its

BARTHELME THE SCRIVENER

transience and its preservation solely in the repetitive form of memory.

"Daumier," the concluding story in *Sadness*, reinforces the need to connect the imaginative with the everyday world by examining the attempt to escape not from an unsympathetic public but from the desire, at once limitless and limited, which is to say the authentic configuration of the self. Daumier, the central figure, whose name evokes that of the great nineteenth century French master of caricature, describes himself as a "tourist of the emotions." He projects two fictive alter egos, or surrogates as he calls them. Both, he acknowledges, are designed to permit a distraction of "the original, authentic self, which is a dirty great villain, as can be testitifed and sworn to by anyone who has every been awake" (*S* 163). In contrast to that self, villainous because insatiable, the surrogates are in principle, satiable, which is to say, can be designed with adventures that are brought to an end. The ambition to structure art in this way proves an example of the narrator's hubris and meets an appropriately ironic fate when the narrator ultimately opens his own world to that of one of his fictive creations.

Arranged in a series of disconnected passages, each of which, like a Victorian novel, is headed by a brief description of its contents or of the action to come, the story leads to levels within fictive levels, complicated even further by allusions to several genres—the western, the historical romance, the domestic comedy, and the story within a story among them. Often these become literalized metaphors. When the original Daumier comments that one of his surrogates rides "the plains and pampas of [his] consciousness," the following scene takes place on just such a location. When he imagines a scene in his mind's eye, he goes on to imagine a mind's neck as well.

There are frequent indications these inventions are to be responded to as pictures rather than as narrative. Along with abrupt shifts, lists, passages of literary quotation, or mixtures of highly stylized and colloquial diction that interrupt the narrative to confirm its artificiality; the situations themselves, as John Ditsky among others has noted, are self-consciously pictorial, a device Barthelme employs to undermine the authority of plot.[10] Rather than suggest the relation between the various elements of the story, the compositional effect is highly ironic. In one passage, for example, a fictive possibility is translated into a literal situation:

Two men in horse-riding clothes stood upon a plain, their attitudes indicating close acquaintance or colleagueship. The plain presented in its foreground a heavy yellow oblong salt lick rendered sculptural by the attentions over a period of time of sheep or other salt-loving animals. Two horses in the situation's upper lefthand corner watched the men with nervous horse-gaze (S 165).

BARTHELME THE SCRIVENER

Daumier himself engages in a discussion of this fictive strategy with a friend named Gibbon, who attributes his comparatively untroubled sense of self-worth to his having been raised without the use of irony. Gibbon, however, confesses finally that he doesn't have enough money to pay for the drinks the two men are having and, in fact, can offer only the bizarre alternative of Krishna Socialism as an alternative to fiction as a means of meliorating the anxieties which trouble both men and presumably everyone else as well.

Unlike the satiability of his surrogates, the narrator's claim of impersonality, proves spurious. As in "The Balloon," he intrudes to acknowledge the function of the story as compensatory. Then, literally folding his characters away in tissue paper, he underscores their flatness and their fragility. It is, in fact, one of the surrogates who provides him with a formula that applies to his fictive existence and through it to the enveloping idea of fiction as well. "There are always openings, if you can find them," a second Daumier promises, "there is always something to do" (*S* 179). The promise comes at a time when the original Daumier finds himself at a dead end in his life no less than in his fiction. His romantic attachments seem to last exactly two years; his hope of doing something great "perhaps in the field of popular music, or light entertainment in general" is shadowed by the sense of his own mortality. "You eye the bed, the record-player, the pictures," he thinks, "already making lists of who will take what" (*S* 179).

UNDERSTANDING DONALD BARTHELME

By plunging the self into comically proliferating openings, Barthelme struggles against what one of the surrogates, perhaps in at least partial self-justification, calls "the cocoon of habituation." At the same time, he exposes the artificiality of the strategy the artist employs in an attempt to separate the story from autobiography. What needs to be remembered is that the strategy Daumier adopts is one of replication rather than novelty, one whose force, as his companion Amelia skeptically seems to be aware, rests, if anything, in a more realistic assessment of possibilities than Daumier is prepared to admit. If the self is to be reassured, or, as Daumier proposes, at least distracted, conviction must come from the energy and movement of the city itself. Barthelme conveys this movement in a descriptive passage that further complicates the narrative's fantastic mingling of plots. Daumier imagines a surrogate and his cowboy band driving a herd of *au-pair* girls into a life of white slavery pursued by Ignatius Loyola and "a band of hard-riding fanatical Jesuits" who hope to rescue the girls. This plot is complicated by the unexplained arrival of a musketeer from a Dumas's novel, who needs help in retrieving the Queen's necklace. An interruption, headed "Description of Three O'Clock in the Afternoon," adds a further level of reality (or unreality). Characteristically, Barthelme combines baroque diction with a specificity of detail in the following extract that needs to be quoted at length:

BARTHELME THE SCRIVENER

Dispersed amidst the hurly and burly of the children were their tenders, shouting. Inmixed with this broil were ordinary denizens of the quarter—shopmen, *rentiers*, churls, sellers of vicious drugs, stum-drinkers, aunties, girls whose jeans had been improved with applique rose blossoms in the cleft of the buttocks, practicers of the priest hustle, and the like. Two officers of the Shore Patrol were hitting an imbecile Sea Scout with long shapely well-modeled nightsticks under the impression that they had jurisdiction. A man was swearing fine-sounding swearwords at a small yellow motorcar of Italian extraction, the same having joined its bumper to another bumper, the two bumpers intertangling like shameless lovers in the act of love. A man in the organic-vegetable hustle stood in the back of a truck praising tomatoes, the same being abulge with tomato-muscle and ablaze with minimum daily requirements. Several members of the madman profession made the air sweet with their imprecating and their moans and the subtle music of the tearing of their hair (*S* 168).

Despite the aimlessnes, the density, the messiness of the scene, really because of them, a vitality emerges from the very surface of events—the listing rather than dramatization—in a catalog that copies and so reminds, even assures the reader of activity and so creates it into being. At length, Daumier becomes so entranced with his creations that he allows Celeste, one of the *au-pair* girls, to replace his real-life companion Amelia in his affections and literally to enter the world in which he

exists. The ontological confusion of levels ends with
Daumier anticipating a meal Celeste is about to prepare,
which in its wonderful elegance recalls the irrelevance
which the narrator of "The Party" felt marked the attempt to discriminate among critical values. Though
Daumier repeats the reassurance given by his surrogate—"There are always openings, if you can find
them. There is always something to do." (S 177)—the
qualification "if you can find them" suggests he is aware
of both the tentative and tenuous nature of such options. Both distancing himself from and embracing his
creations, then, he confirms by his act both the need to,
and the means by which fiction can, enter the world and
the ambiguous condition that results when it does so.

Many of the concerns Barthelme expressed in *Sadness* appear again in his next collection of short stories,
Amateurs, where they are often subjected to more manic
treatment. In "Our Work and Why We Do It," the narrator describes the operations of a publishing house
which serves as the center of a series of bizarre, unrelated activities, somewhat resembling the acts in "The
Flight of Pigeons from the Palace." The owners, William
and Rowena, lie naked in bed in the middle of the plant
discoursing on the advantages of being bourgeois,
which allows William to worry about his plants and his
quiches, his property taxes, and, in a stunning incongruity, his sword hilt. The pressmen turn out jobs ranging from matchbook covers to the *Oxford Book of
American Grub* and the Detroit telephone book, while

awaiting the introduction of new machines which will print underground telephone poles, the smoke on smoked hams, and the figure 5 in gold. "Should we smash the form?" one of the pressmen wonders when a job receives a bad review, then realizes "But it's *our* form" (*A* 7).

It is an exchange it is not hard to imagine the author having with himself. In the absence of conventional forms (and perhaps the occasional impulse to smash them), the story serves as a paradigm of Barthelme's work and suggests why he does it. The narrator is unable to end some of his sentences and begins others seemingly in the middle, punctuating both with occasional non sequiturs, lists, and even an obscurely threatening note wrapped around a brick that sails through the window and identifies conditions without indicating the consequences. "And I saw the figure 5 writ in gold," is one of the statements he abruptly introduces. The allusion is to a painting by Charles DeMuth, inspired by William Carlos Williams's Imagist poem "The Great Figure." Though a symbolic homage to the poet, whose name and initials are worked into it, the painting is done in the hard-edge style of the precisionists, a group of artists including Charles Sheeler and Stuart Davis with whom Demuth is commonly grouped and who painted everyday themes and common household objects—grain elevators, barns, silos, factories, ship's turbines—in an attempt to reduce and simplify natural forms to the borderline of abstraction. It is a style that in many ways seems to anticipate Barthelme's own. "Some things don't make sense," the narrator explains of the rush of words that can be seen finally as the subject of the story:

But that isn't our job, to make sense of things—our job is to kiss the paper with the form or plate, as the case may be, and make sure it's not getting too much ink, and worry about the dot structure of the engravings, or whether a tiny shim is going to work up during the run and split a fountain (*A* 5).

The process of the story not its content is what the reader is instructed to pay attention to.

In "The Captured Woman" a similarly improbable situation results from the transformation into literal terms of the vocabulary of power and sexual domination commonly used to describe relationships. The narrator and his friends boast of their methods (one uses tranquilizing darts, another a lasso, a third a spell inherited from his great-grandmother; the narrator uses Jack Daniels) and of their success in taming the women they have captured. Like the domestic situations the women have left, these more exotic arrangements after a while come to seem "as ordinary as bread," and, though the narrator feels they are are at best temporary, over the course of time they take on a permanence as the women

BARTHELME THE SCRIVENER

at first subtly and then more agressively use their supposedly dependent status to gain control of the relationship.

Control operates as the informing principle of "I Bought a Little City," which also literalizes then reverses the wish-fulfillment conditions with which it begins. The city which the narrator buys, Galveston, Texas, is treated as though it were a sports franchise run by a benevolent owner. Starting with some modest urban renewal, he tears down an entire city block and converts it into a park. "I put the people into the Galvez Hotel, which is the nicest hotel in town, right on the seawall," the narrator drawls full of self-satisfaction, "and I made sure that every room had a beautiful view. Those people had wanted to stay at the Galvez Hotel all their lives and never had a chance before because they didn't have the money. They were delighted" (*A* 52). Predictably the satisfaction fades with the problems of relocation and the increasingly arbitrary changes the narrator makes (partly in response to the citizens' requests) in an effort to convert his city into a utopian dream. The result is a fragmented jigsaw puzzle which pleases no one. The attempt to bring order to the city is no more successful and when the narrator is rebuffed by one of the married women who live there he decides to sell it back at a loss. By attempting to be imaginative one can only hurt people, not help them, he concludes. It is a way of playing God, whose more powerful and painful imagination causes him to withdraw from society completely, still tormented by the thought of the wife whose fidelity could not be tempted.

Barthelme reverses that situation in "You Are as Brave as Vincent van Gogh," which deals with the desperate reassurances that attempt to keep an affair from falling apart, and in "The Agreement," "What to Do Next," and more obliquely, in "At the End of the Mechanical Age," all of which seem more nakedly informed by a personal voice struggling with the problem of divorce and its aftermath. In "The Agreement," the divorced speaker, as in a catechism, asks himself a series of searing questions beginning with "Where is my daughter? Why is she there? What crucial error did I make? Was there more than one?" (*A* 61). Concerned as well about social approval (Will the mailman laugh at him? The butcher? The doctor?), he worries about his lover's fidelity and his own competence. The narrator's self-questioning is abruptly ended by a parody of one of the terms of a supposed divorce agreement, covering every conceivable contingency "from the beginning of the world to the execution of this agreement." Having agreed to the terms of this document, he finds the loss and dislocation intrude upon his efforts to get on with the painting of his apartment and the beginning of a new life it promises.

"What to Do Next," consists of ostensible instructions for what the narrator ironically terms "starting fresh, as it is called" after a couple has separated. In-

itially comparing the experiences to the loss of one's
dog, he at first advises distractions to help one forget
the depression but quickly recognizes that such diversions do little to address the central difficulty: the loss
of self-esteem. The narrator traces such "wrenches of
the spirit," to the culture which, he recognizes, "makes
of us all either machines for assimilating and judging
that culture, or uncritical sops who simply sop it up,
become it" (*A* 85). The image of separation from one's
culture—that of a banged thumb, swollen and red—is,
however, no more appealing. His solution, which he
compares to "frontier-busting," is to become part of the
instructions themselves or in other words to write about
the experience just as he himself is doing. Even this
strategy is viewed ironically. Along with the instructions the newly authoritative divorcee is required to
give a course twelve hours a week to others seeking
solace for which the instructor will receive three credits
and a silver spoon in the Heritage pattern. "The anthol-
ogy of yourself which will be used as a text," the narrator hollowly reassures the reader, "is even now being
assembled by underpaid researchers in our textbook di-
vision" (*S* 86) and underscores the ambivalent irony he
directs at these mechanical means for dealing with the
pain of loss by concluding the instructions with the
words, "Congratulations. I'm sorry" (*S* 86).

Toward the middle of "At the End of the Mechanical Age," the narrator wonders whether the end of the
mechanical age, which he equates with the present age

of electricity, is simply a metaphor. "We have a duty to understand everything," he is told, at which point the boat, in which he and his companion have been riding out a flood which followed forty days and forty nights of rain, sinks. His companion, Mrs. Davis, had reached out to him in a grocery store and following extravagant promises of idealized romantic fulfillment which both are aware can never be realized, they marry. His ideal had been a woman named Maude, who, as in Barthelme's own fiction, attempts to create things by naming them. Mrs. Davis's fantasy is that of a natty dresser with many credit cards who bears a resemblance to her first husband, Jake. The wedding turns the metaphor into reality with the mechanical nature of the ceremony:

"And do you, Anne," the minister said, "promise to make whatever mutually satisfactory accommodations necessary to reduce tensions and arrive at whatever previously agreed-upon goals both parties have harmoniously set in the appropriate planning sessions?" (*A* 181).

The accommodations set the tone of the relationship, and despite the narrator's appeal for the blessing of some Divine Presence, which ironically had been hovering behind everything that has happened, the marriage ends in a divorce which along with "blackouts, brownouts, temporary dimmings of household illumination" only confirms divine indifference. God, the narrator concludes bitterly, is "interested only in grace—in keeping things humming" (*A* 183). The ending of the story once more combines the compromises demanded by the world and the more abstract truths of metaphor. Neither Mrs. Davis nor the narrator appear discouraged by the need to find happiness without the aid of some supernatural being. Their child goes to live in Russia where, the narrator believes, "He is probably growing in wisdom and beauty." With "the glow of hope not yet extinguished, the fear of pall not yet triumphant" the couple continues to search for an ideal, but only with the aid of standby generators which ensure the flow of grace.

Like the writer in "The Dolt," whose story lacked a middle, the narrator of "And Then" struggles with metaphors and with the difficulty of completing his own fiction. "The part of the story that came next was suddenly missing," he begins (*S* 105) and then goes on to imagine a series of increasingly fantastic encounters with a public which appears to him in the form of an obscurely threatening policeman who comically multiplies (or divides) into several more, all with bicycles, demanding that he turn over a harpsichord he had given to his wife as a present. Only by lying, the narrator decides, can he successfully distract this looming presence, and desperately looking for ways to keep his audience interested he becomes lost in his own inventions. The two problems—satisfying the audience and completing his story—thus fuse into one, which he plans to resolve with an extravagant gesture. He will throw chicken livers *flambé* all over the predicament. "That," he concludes hopefully, "will 'open up' the situation successfully. I will resolve these terrible contradictions with flaming chicken parts and then sing the song of how I contrived the ruin of my anaconda" (*A* 112).

As a means of resolving the predicament of both artist and audience, the spontaneous gesture proves a fragile solution in "The Great Hug," a story which returns to the central metaphor of "The Balloon." Summoned to console a companion to whom the narrator has given some terminally bad news, the Balloon Man appears like a carnival huckster with an assortment of balloons of all colors and varieties. They range from the Balloon of Not Yet and the Balloon of Sometimes to the Balloon of Perhaps, which the story concludes, is his best balloon. Unwilling to have his picture taken because he "doesn't want the others to steal his moves," the Balloon Man explains "It's all in the gesture—the precise, reunpremeditated right move" (*A* 46). Although the balloons do not lie, the reader is told, the Balloon Man is less straightforward than the Pin Lady, his antagonist, who presents an actuality with which his imaginative creations must ultimately be locked. His balloons, or the stories with which they are associated, at best thus provide only qualified or temporary refuge in dealing with reality. Referring to the scene with which the story begins, the narrator says "When he created our butter-colored balloon, we felt better," then adds thoughtfully, "a little better" (*A* 48). Yet the Balloon Man defends with spirit the qualified nature of one's encounter with his product. "Not every balloon can make you happy," the Balloon Man admits, "Not every balloon can trigger glee. *But I insist that these balloon have a right to be heard!*" (*A* 48).

Nearly half of the sixteen stories in *Great Days* take this insistence literally, by concentrating in dialogue form on the sound of language. Barthelme has described this contrapuntal technique as an attempt through the arrangement of words to arrive at new meanings rather than simply providing an altered perspective in which to regard them.[11] In fact, the use exclusively of dialogue as a framing device allows Barthelme to reduce the story to its basic dramatic element eliminating for the most part such narrative elements as plot, description, development, and even climax. Unlike the adversarial debates of "The Explanation" or "Kierkegaard Unfair to Schlegel," in *City Life*, or even the more playful story, "The Reference" in *Amateurs* (in which the exchange takes place between a stuffy, jargon-spouting prospective employer whose difficulties with social engineering have resulted in "planarchy" and a slangy, jive-talking antagonist whose often meaningless patter evolves into that of an agent's, representing the person for whom the reference is sought), the voices in *Great Days* are more like syncopated duets.

Structured like the classic jazz tune "Momma Don't

'Low," with its refrain and improvisations, "The New Music" develops the conversation of two brothers who have difficulty in liberating themselves from the influence of a repressive, largely unfeeling mother. Once again the parallels with an authoritative artistic tradition suggest themselves. Ironically the conversation begins with the admission by one of the brothers of imitation in a surprising context. Asked what he did that day, he replies, "Went to the grocery store and Xeroxed a box of English muffins, two pounds of ground veal and an apple. In flagrant violation of the Copyright Act" (*GD* 21). Their discussion of the new music is, in actuality, an example of it, touching on both its eclectic quality and its almost syncopated rhythms:

—If one does nothing but listen to the new music, everything else drifts, goes away, frays. Did Odysseus feel this way when he and Diomedes decided to steal Athene's statue from the Trojans, so that they would become dejected and lose the war? I don't think so, but who is to know what effect the new music of that remote time had on its hearers?
—Or how it compares to the new music of this time?
—One can only conjecture (*GD* 21–2)

Alternately building on and echoing each other's remarks, the brothers remind each other of all the prohibitions to which they have been subjected and which

BARTHELME THE SCRIVENER

spill over from their musical interests to their social lives. Their attempt to reassure themselves with brave resolutions ("Get my ocarina tuned, sew a button on my shirt." "Got to air my sleeping bag, scrub up my canteen.") centers around a vision of the utopian city of Pool, which, it turns out, only projects a dated image of itself obtained from movies that seem made of standard film clichés.

Despite the discouragement they feel at the prospect of getting older and the intimidating influence of official statements such as that of *The Hite Report*, a study of female sexuality, the brothers' conversation itself finally proves sustaining, even revitalizing. Like the new music, which has no steady beat ("The new music is drumless, which is brave)." *GD* 33), the conversation renews itself by accommodating a wide range of subjects from Greek mythology and poetry of the French symbolists to discos and mixed drinks. "The new music," one of the brothers says, "burns things together, like a welder." At the same time, its colloquial rhythms resemble "the new, down-to-earth, think-I'm-gonna-kill-myself music, which unwraps the sky" (*GD* 37). Despite its echo of Shakespearian tragedy in the recognition that "the new music will be there tomorrow and tomorrow and tomorrow," the brothers are convinced, at length, that they can deal with the prospect of things coming to an end and the troubling dreams which are certain to follow by abandoning the prospect of utopian dreams and confining themselves to a new music whose novelty depends, above all, simply on routine mainte-nance.

Elliptical jazz rhythms also structure the conversa-tion in "Morning," in which two men similarly attempt to confront the terrors of aging and loss as they are brought home in the early light of another day. "Say you're frightened. Admit it," one begins. "I watch my hand aging," the other replies with an unconvincing attempt at casual bravery, "sing a little song" (*GD* 123). The song consists in the main of disconnected riffs which include imitations by one of them of the lonliness in the cry of a wolf and appeals to literary and artistic diversions. "What shall we do? Call up Mowgli? Ask him over? . . . Is Scriabin as smart as he looks?" (*GD* 123).

The two men attempt to comfort themselves with formulaic, singsong repetitions ("One old man alone in a room. Two old men alone in a room. Three old men alone in a room."), by mocking allusions to familiar catchphrases ("Have any of the English residents been murdered?"), and by humorous variations of classic song titles ("They played 'One O'Clock Jump,' 'Two O'Clock Jump,' 'Three O'Clock Jump,' and 'Four O'Clock Jump.'") Without the awareness of them as a strategy, the reassurances prove hollow, remaining ab-stractions rather than acquiring density. The story ends not with the expected daylight but with darkness and the abandoning of the search for any pleasurable or even satisfying illumination.

A parallel pessimism informs the conversation in "On the Steps of the Conservatory," which describes one woman's rejection by a Conservatory, whose standards remain arbitrary and whose function is never made clear. What is known is only that the Conservatory "is hostile to the new spirit." Without identifying in explicit terms which institution the Conservatory is identified with (in one sense it parallels the non-permissive momma in "The New Music"), its syllabus reveals a traditional concern for image rather than substance. "Christian imagery is taught at the Conservatory, also Islamic imagery and the imagery of Public Safety," Hilda explains to her friend Maggie (*GD* 134). Like everything else, however, even the image of the conservatory itself continues to shift. Initially its staff is described as indifferent to the models, subsequently as sexually involved with them. Even Maggie does not remain a fixed entity, speaking alternately in her own voice, which repeatedly reminds Hilda of her pregnant condition and as a spokeswoman for the conservatory, who delights in pointing out the privileges to which Hilda will never be entitled. The conversation ends with Maggie's suggestion that even her intermittent attempt at consolation, like Hilda's tenuous effort to cope with her rejection, is questionable and that jealousy and envy rather than support underlies the nature of the women's relationship.

The same irony is evident in the abstract conversation of the two unnamed women in "Great Days," which, unlike the dialogues between two women in *The Dead Father* that preceded the story and that it otherwise resembles, was, according to Barthelme, a more concrete experiment in combinations that could keep the reader interested without a strong narrative line on which to lean.[12] In "Great Days," the voices of two women are projected against the menacing background of crime reports that sound like broadcasts on an urban police radio frequency, both repetitive and discontinuous. The women worry about growing older, their fading beauty, their uncertain achievements. They attempt to reassure each other with meaningless sentiments from popular song lyrics or current catch-phrases expressing popular wisdom, while hoping for the child-like renewal associated with rainwashed watercolors. "Control used to be the thing," one of them decides, "Now abandon" (*GD* 166). In part, the voices constitute a parody of Barthelme's reductive style, bouncing off of, though never quite responding to, what one says to the other. Yet the staccato, elliptical rhythm of their conversation is illuminated by the description one of them gives of her own painting style which is marked by her efforts to "get my colors together. Trying to play one off against another. Trying for cancellation" (*GD* 159).

BARTHELME THE SCRIVENER

The style is Barthelme's as well, and the effort at cancellation expands into a more general statement that is not directed at any identifiable object or made in response to any specific comment but seems to express Barthelme's view of art: a "nonculminating kind of ultimately affectless activity" one of the women calls it (*GD* 159). Neither focused by some controlling purpose nor generating some precise emotion, it is just that kind of aimless activity the women think of as the great days of their lives filled with concrete if transitory everyday moments of childlike playfulness and enveloping sensory experience. Making mud pies, eating ice cream, singing, they recall, the days were "all perfect and ordinary and perfect" (*GD* 157). The loss of those days occasions in the women as adults an insatiable need for reassurance and a consequent mistrust of the attempt or even the ability either of lovers or friends to provide it.

Reassurance is also sought in "The Leap," a story in which antiphonal responses alternate with shifting tonal modulations and philosophies to make it appear the two voices the reader hears are contesting sides of a single personality. Cheered by "the wine of possibility," one speaker attempts to persuade his companion to make the leap of faith, but only after each has carefully reexamined his conscience and acknowledged the failings it reminds him of. The force of this religious argument is mockingly challenged by the other voice, that of a self-styled double-minded man who wonders whether "He wants us to grovel quite so much?" "I don't think He gives a rap," his friend replies, "But it's traditional" (*GD* 151).

The ludicrous consequences of too strict an observance of tradition is suggested by the doubter's insistence on regarding his sins item by item. His mock humility prompts the first speaker to express a hierarchy of values that proves both arbitrary and comically restrictive in its fine discriminations. "I like people better than plants," he points out, "plants better than animals, paintings better than animals, and music better than animals" (*GD* 147). This list contrasts with a more comprehensive idea of the sublime to which both men enthusiastically subscribe, one that does not discriminate among alternatives but celebrates the rich variety of earthly phenomena, from a glass of water or the joy of looking at "a woman with really red hair" to the beauty of the human voice. In contrast to the evidence of some religious meaning in existence, the men comment on the human creative impulse responsible for the most banal works of art, the childlike regularity of which both men underscore by alternately quoting the lines of Joyce Kilmer's "Trees," along with the typographical appearance of the lines on the page. ("'I think that I shall never see slash A poem lovely as a tree.'")

Rehearsing the torments of the damned as they are typically phrased in sermons, the two men suggest yet another motive for the leap of faith. Here the man who would make the leap seems to take on the posture of his double-minded antagonist. Reminded of the philosophical argument that "purity of heart is to will one thing" he replies, "No. Here I differ with Kierkegaard. Purity of heart is, rather, to will several things, and not know which is the better, truer thing, and to worry about this, forever" (*GD* 151). In its complexity, the statement suggests something of the skepticism or hesitancy that inhibits the will to believe. In its concern and consequent anxieties, it points to the urgency of precisely that need and the correlative desire for reassurance.

The two men agree that the divine plan is artificial in its established forms and suspect as it appears to work itself out in the inability of nations to achieve zero population growth or in such individual acts of self-destruction as suicide—a leap away from faith, the first speaker admits—and the impersonal way society deals with it as evidenced by an itemized hospital bill. Nonetheless they acknowledge evidence of the plan can be found in the example of love in all its complexity. "Is it *permitted* to differ with Kierkegaard?" the double-minded man wonders. "Not only permitted," he is assured, "but necessary. If you love him," (*GD* 152).

With this realization of complexity, even in love, the first speaker concludes by sharing his friend's abruptly confessed inability to make the leap of faith or at least his willingness to delay it and so becomes more in need of reassurance than ever. He finds that reassurance in the appreciation of the chaotic but nonetheless sublime quality of concrete experience in its ordinary forms. "A wedding day," he suggests. "A plain day," the double-minded man corrects him, bringing to his uncertainty a measure not only of comfort but of hope.

The broken rhythms of the dialogue stories find an echo not only in the voices of "The King of Jazz" but in the art of its central figure, the trombone player Hokie Mokie who, Barthelme has acknowledged, reflects his interest in the legendary jazz musicians of the 1930s, whose skill at improvisation served as a model for the writer's own strategy of renewing familiar material by unexpected placement of emphasis or by introducing elaborate variations of it. "You'd hear some of these guys take a tired old tune like 'Who's Sorry Now?'" Barthelme told one interviewer, "and do the most incredible things with it, make it beautiful, literally make it new. The interest and the drama were in the formal manipulation of the rather slight material."[13] The material in "The King of Jazz" recounts the challenge to the newly crowned king, Hokie Mokie, from the Japanese jazz man Hideo Yamaguchi. After an initial performance, Hokie is forced to acknowledge the superiority of Hideo's playing, but in a subsequent encounter Hokie's inspired playing allows him to reclaim his crown, sending Hideo back to Japan with the knowledge of "many years of work and study before me still." Barthelme takes the opportunity to make fun both of the dated critical vocabulary to which the artist's performance is subjected and the exaggerated enthusiasms it generates. Ironically harking back to the categories of modernism, Hokie's playing is described as having "the real epiphanic glow," while Hideo's peculiar way of holding his horn prompts the supposedly knowledgeable observation, "That's frequently the mark of a superior player." Even Hokie's naming of the tune the band will play is greeted with syncophantic adulation: "'Wow'!" everybody said. "'Did you hear that? Hokie Mokie can just knock a fella out, just the way he pronounces a word. What a intonation on that boy! God Almighty!'" (*GD* 56). At length, a description of Hokie's playing yields an improvisation of its own, which parallels the music it attempts to describe and brings together in an ambivalent tone the truly heroic nature of the art and, for Barthelme, the finally inescapable extravagance with which it is greeted. Called upon to identify Hokie's sound, one of the audience supplies the following similes:

"You mean that sound that sounds like the cutting edge of life? That sounds like polar bears crossing Arctic ice pans? That sounds like a herd of musk ox in full flight? That sounds like male walruses diving to the bottom of the sea? That sounds like fumaroles smoking on the slopes of Mt. Katmai? That sounds like the wild turkey walking through the deep, soft forest? That sounds like beavers chewing trees in the Appalachian marsh? . . ." (*GD* 59).

The speaker continues to add to the list growing wilder and wilder as he goes on. Unable to end, he is brought to a stop only when he is interrupted by the observation, perhaps meant to shape his own jazzy flights, that Hokie is playing with a mute.

A different sort of performance becomes the subject of "The Death of Edward Lear," whose hero literally transforms the moment of his death into a vibrant and enduring performance with a life of its own. The situation, dreamlike in its associational logic—the displacement of emotion, and the neutralization of time and space—draws its meaning, like dreams, from the intention of the dreamer, that is to say, from the enactment of his desire rather than the revelatory content of images. This is not to suggest that in Barthelme's fiction history has no meaning; it is to say that imagination brings with it its own deceptions or, more accurately, establishes its own myths. The sources of these myths are found in public, or shared, as well as private visions. Lear invites his public to witness his death, which they prepare to attend with all the confusion and excitement that would accompany their spending a day in the country, but from which they come away "agreed that, all in all, it had been a somewhat tedious performance (*GD* 103). Subsequently repertory companies reenact the death scene, which in the course of time, they modify to portray Lear "shouting, shaking, vibrant with rage." These revivals thus lose sight of the author's intention and, in the process, of his originality and charm. In the whimsical and arbitrary nature of his final acts, the narrator explains, "Mr. Lear had been doing what he had always done and therefore, not doing anything extraordinary. Mr. Lear had transformed the extraordinary into its opposite. He had, in point of fact, created a gentle, genial misunderstanding" (*GD* 103).

In "Cortes and Montezuma," events resist interpretation in part because of the distortions that occur when different civilizations view each other's customs solely from the limited perspective provided by their own. Eating white bread appears just as cannibalistic to the Incan culture as human flesh does to the Spanish. Each regards the other's religious practices as equally perverse. "That the Son should be sacrificed," Montezuma tells Cortes, "seems to me wrong. It seems to me He should be sacrificed *to*" (*GD* 46). Cortes responds by replacing an image of the god Blue Hummingbird with one of the Virgin. In more secular terms, Montezuma defines the role of the ruler in a way that parallels the artist Barthelme describes in stories such as "The Balloon," or, more obliquely, "The Glass Mountain": he prepares dramas that make it easier for both himself and his subjects to face "the prospect of world collapse, the prospect of the world folding in upon itself . . ." (*GD* 47).

It is fiction, however, not the world which threatens to fold in upon itself. Structured in disconnected scenes whose details make them highly visual but which impose strict limits on its own thematic organization, the narrative does not allow the reader to move easily from one episode to the next but rather keeps attention focused on a single action at a time, often as it occurs within a single paragraph. Like the annoying green flies, whose ubiquitous presence is unaccounted for other than as a reminder of a nagging commonplace reality, anachronistic references insistently disrupt the conventional relation between history and invention. "What's he been up to?" Cortes asks in current slang about a member of his expedition while the translator, Dona Marina, walks with one hand tucked inside the belt of her Incan lover, at the back, like a contemporary couple strolling through Greenwich Village. Allusions are made to private detectives, home movies, and to words such as "guillotine," "temperament," "entitlement," "*schnell*," some of which have yet to be coined, all of which are clearly out of place in the context of Incan culture.

The attempt throughout, then, is to reduce the mythic stature of these figures to a more human if still unfamiliar history, whose sudden and surprising turns are illustrated in the person of Bernal Diaz del Castillo, who, the reader is told, will one day write a *True History of the Conquest of New Spain*. Bernal is pictured as whittling on a piece of mesquite as though passing a long afternoon telling stories on the porch of a southwest country store. Looked at in one way, these incongruous juxtapositions deflate the fabulous element of the narrative; in another they become themselves magically predictive in the sense indicated by the narrator of "Paraguay" of that mixture of invention and reality.

This tension, typical of Barthelme's fiction, is not limited to linguistic content but rather works its way out from the center of the story—the intimate treatment of legendary figures whose history has become obscured by the mythic significance, in part slyly internalized, to which it has become attached. The same ominous omens—lightning and rain sweeping off the lake—accompany insignificant events such as the building of a chicken coop as well as those of historical importance such as the murder of the Incan ruler. The mixture of levels is similarly illustrated in the Spaniards' search for treasure, which results in the discovery of mummified animals concealed behind a wall but also yields a "puddle" of gold. Both the sound and the meaning of the word "puddle" suggest the banality of experience. Contextually associated with gold, it becomes invested with a more magical sense.

The literal acceptance of even the most unlikely conjunctions is, perhaps, most forcefully conveyed by the uninflected tone used to describe the exchange between the two political antagonists as a variation of the relation between lovers. Cortes and Montezuma hold hands, exchange useless gifts, spy jealously on one another, finally give way to acts of betrayal and scenes of recrimination. Like the course of events, even the imaginative forms through which the two men attempt to anticipate and so understand them remain outside their control. In a concluding ghostly confrontation, Montezuma reproaches his friend for failing to alter the outcome of a dream which Cortes did not have and which he did not even appear in. "I did what I thought best," Cortes had earlier explained to the Emperor Charles of Spain, "proceeding with gaiety and conscience." It is Montezuma who unaccountably replies, "I am murdered" (*GD* 51). It is the gaiety to which the reader is particularly directed. Without it, as one learns from the two often stand-up-comic voices exchanging questions and replies in "Kierkegaard Unfair to Schlegel," one has nothing with which to face the "imbecile questions," which look for a pattern in life, the unsatisfying answers, and the inescapable fact that things appear to lead nowhere.

All art, the reader can infer, takes as its informing purpose, the attempt to express "the possible plus two," which is found in the example of the 400,000 welded steel artichokes constructed by the artist-hero of "The Abduction from the Seraglio." In doing so, however, it must follow the example in that story of the artist's former girlfriend, Costanze, who does not compromise her values by her decision to move in with a wealthy car dealer but who continues to live "in a delicate relation to the real." And though the artist has lost his muse to the attractions held out by the Plymouth Dealer, who updates Mozart's Pasha as a representative (though somewhat less benevolent) of a self-indulgent

society, he pronounces this qualified though still ultimately upbeat benediction: "We adventured. That's not
bad" (*GD* 95).

Published in 1983, *Overnight to Many Distant Cities,*
Barthelme's eighth volume of short fiction is, in many
ways, his most innovative collection. Several of
Barthelme's familiar themes are easily recognizable,
among them the anxieties of urban life, the fragility of
domestic arrangements, the transience of romance, the
qualities of sadness and beauty that inform the awareness of time, and the moments of perceived vitality that
mark as luminous its passage. Yet the 12 stories that
make up the volume take on a less ironic, more personal
voice than that which typically marks Barthelme's earlier work. These full-length stories are counterpointed
by the inclusion of brief (typically no more than 2 or 3
pages), italicized interchapters, which adopt a tone of
nuanced sophistication that challenges the conventional
relations between the order of things and the order of
words, challenges, that is, the different ways in which
structure or fictive order is imposed upon the dizzying
impact of experience. In one of them, for example, two
women, described as gift-wrapped, are initially pictured
wearing nothing but web belts to which canteens are
attached. The women appear in a succession of situations initially located in the indeterminate space of a
performance art work by Yves Klein ("Nowhere—the
middle of it, its exact center").[14] Subsequently the scene

shifts to an architectural office where they sit before a pair of drafting tables, a lumberyard in southern Illinois, the composing room of an Akron, Ohio, newspaper, New York City, where they appear first as taxi drivers then as loan officers in a bank, and finally to an archeological dig in the Cameroons. Intermittently the women excite satyr-like young men who "squirm and dance under this treatment, hanging from hooks, while giant eggs, seated in red plush chairs, boil" (*O* 70). Figures ranging from the Russian artist Vladimir Tatlin in an asbestos tuxedo to Benvenuto Cellini and the French painter Georges de La Tour, both wearing white overalls, appear in the background. The surreal quality of the images (La Tour, who watches the women in a film, is subsequently pictured in the lobby of the theater opening a bag of M&Ms with his teeth) prohibits any interpretation other than to suggest that women, particularly in their nakedness, constitute somewhat troublesome gifts and also breathtaking works of art that are drawn from the most representative kinds of experience.

The sly undercutting of the ideal is directed toward art no less than life in the first interchapter of the volume which envisions a utopian city much like that of Barthelme's earlier story "Paraguay," and begins abruptly with the narrator's remark, "They called for more structure, then . . ." (*O* 9). There is no indication of who has made the request, what kind of structure is required, or even the nature of what has already been built. While the story is filled with a wide range of contemporary allusions, none appear in recognizable contexts or satisfy conventional expectations so that it is not so much another world that is glimpsed as this one slightly out of focus. Clad in red Lego, for example, the city is spread out in the shape of the word FASTIGIUM, which proves to be not its name but a set of letters selected for the elegance of the script. Even the structure which follows the initial request is achieved by the use of materials with surprising characteristics—"big hairy four-by-fours [are nailed] into place with railroad spikes" (O 9) while the impermanence of the whole is suggested by specified areas designed to decay and so return in time to open space.

The fluid architectural design serves equally as a paradigm of Barthelme's own fiction in which the elements of fantasy do not so much displace or even alternate with reality as exist side by side with it. In another interchapter, the narrator puts a name in an envelope which, like a children's counting song, he continues to expand until the succession of envelopes and objects stuffed into them includes the Victoria and Albert Museum, the Royal Danish Ballet, boric acid, and the entire history of art. All are compressed into a new blue suit which walks away on its own, an action that suggests something of both the compression and the autonomy of art.

The casual acceptance of the bizarre as part of the ordinary lies at the center of yet another interchapter (reprinted in *Forty Stories*, where it is given the title "Pepperoni") which describes in matter-of-fact terms a daily newspaper in which the editorials have been subcontracted to Texas Instruments, the obituaries to Nabisco, and in which the reporters form a chamber orchestra that plays Haydn in the newsroom. The incongruities that mark the running of the paper are highlighted in the selection as the page-one lead of a story on pepperoni—"a useful and exhaustive guide"—run alongside instructions on "slimming-your-troublesome-thighs" with pictures (*O* 25).

Strangely appealing, obscurely menacing, this anti-utopian world in which the trivial takes so prominent a place blends with the everyday in the concluding interchapter, which describes in surrealistic terms, among other things, the decoration of a Christmas tree and a party which possibly follows at which the guests include both thieves and deans of cathedrals. The setting is a magical forest, alive with sensuality and far from Western civilization. In this fairy-tale world in which inanimate objects come to life women at one point partner themselves with large bronze hares (which may also be Christmas tree ornaments) while the narrator's companion jealously regards the already-beautiful who stand watching with various exotic animals cradled in their arms. Despite the unpredictability of events and the tensions to which they seem to give rise, the narrator insists, "This life is better than any I have lived, previously" (*O*164). Even the weather, perhaps the most insistent reminder of the unpredictability of human affairs, continues to be splendid. "It is remarkable," the narrator concludes in what finally appears to be the judgment of the volume, "how well human affairs can be managed, with care" (165).

To such tranquility, however, Barthelme seldom fails to append a cautionary qualification chiefly directed at the relationships which describe much of our contemporary domestic arrangements. In one of the interchapters a wife catalogs the history of a marriage while her husband remains absorbed in the idiosyncratic events chronicled in his newspaper, indifferent even to her complaint that a guest he has brought home occupies himself exclusively with eating mashed potatoes in a back room of their apartment. In "Visitors," the initial full-length story of the volume, Bishop, a divorced father, nearing 50, struggles to bring order to a career which includes caring for a teen-aged daughter visiting at his small apartment during the summer. He must also deal with the end of an idyllic affair with a younger woman and with the various uncertainties and incongruities of city life presented in a catalog that establishes the documentary logic of ennumeration Barthelme typically relies on in place of linear development to structure his narrative. Taking a walk down West Broadway, the narrator encounters "citizens parading, plump-faced and bone-faced, lightly clad. A young black boy toting a Board of Education trombone case. A fellow with oddly-cut hair the color of marigolds and a roll of roofing felt over his shoulder" (16). After Bishop gives his daughter a mock lecture on art, the story concludes with an enigmatic scene he witnesses in an apartment across the way of two old ladies who habitually breakfast by candelight. Bishop cannot decide whether they are incurably romantic or simply trying to save money on electricity, and the alternate interpretations, which serve as well as a paradigm for the responses the story itself invites, suggest the choices no less than the limits which experience simultaneously holds out.

The disconnection that brings to such unusual circumstances a disturbing sense of the commonplace marks the adventures of the eponymous hero of "Captain Blood." "When Captain Blood goes to sea," the story begins, "he locks the doors and windows of his house on Cow Island personally" (*O* 59). Though Blood more exotically keeps marmalade and a spider monkey in his cabin, his pockets are filled with mothballs, and he notes with satisfaction the decorous behavior of his crew. Blood, the buccaneer, is nonetheless plagued by the conventional anxieties of any responsible business entrepreneur. "Should he try another course?" he wonders after a long period during which he is unable to capture any booty, "Another ocean?" (*O* 60) His adventures, which culminate with an unlikely battle in which he first defeats then gallantly frees John Paul Jones, are anchored if not exactly in reality then at least in a more factual illusion by lists that contain a mixture of the

BARTHELME THE SCRIVENER

prosaic and the spectacular. These include the names of the ships he has captured as well as the value of his prizes. Ultimately there is a description of the Catalonian sardana, a dance which, Blood "frequently dances with his men, in the middle of the ocean, after lunch, to the music of a single silver trumpet" (*O* 65). The image of the trumpet evokes a sense of wonder which the wry qualification "after lunch" makes sure to anchor in the requirements of the everyday.

The mystery that informs the everyday continues to resist explanation for Connors, a free-lance journalist in "Lightning," who is given the assignment of interviewing nine people who had been struck by lightning. Middle-aged, barely scraping by after a brief period of affluence, Connors is nonetheless able to reclaim his journalistic integrity only after his wife leaves him for a racquetball pro. He is himself figuratively struck by lightning when, in the course of his assignment, he meets Edwina, a beautiful black model with whom he falls instantly in love. For Edwina, as for the others Connors interviews, it is the pragmatic rather than dramatic effects of the experience that are significant. One man becomes a Jehovah's Witness, another subsequently joins the Nazi Party, a woman subsequently marries a man she had been seeing for two years, a Trappist monk is able to indulge his passion for rock music, and someone dumb from birth is, after being struck, able to begin speaking fluent French. Missing the underlying fact—the lack of drama for the people who must live their lives as subjects of it—Connor is unable to find a common denominator for these experiences and unsuccessfully attempts to impart to them a religious significance. His story, however, both begins and ends with the transient earthly beauty of Edwina, which his editor, Penfield, calls "approximately fantastic." The self-qualifying terms of the description suggest the inexplicable mixture of the extraordinary and the human imperfection which necessarily limits both our approach to and understanding of it and which consequently locates the value of experience in its surface rather than in some transcendent meaning.

In "Affection," emotional intensity similarly emerges less in contrast to the irritating sameness of domestic routine than as a consequence of it. Harris, the husband in a shaky marriage, his wife Claire, his mistress Sarah, all express the need for affection in repetitive appeals whose self-absorbed demands for fulfillment at length merge into a dreamlike blending of figures and relationships. His complaints of infidelity, of sickness, of sexual inadequacy, of the lack of understanding are greeted with indifference, even boredom, by the fortune teller Madame Olympia, who Harris consults only to hear his own domestic quarrels repeated in the experience of her other clients.

The attempt to rehearse the poverty of one's environment is wittily mocked by a T-shirt Madame Olympia wears on which is printed the ironic legend "Buffalo, City of No Illusions." Like Dr. Whorf, the psy-

BARTHELME THE SCRIVENER

chiatrist Sarah consults, Olympia can do little to relieve the misery and estrangement she is told about other than to convert them into cliches. It is the same strategy the story itself employs in a series of melodramatic alternatives intrusively proposed as possibilities for narrative development. "Did they consent to sign it?" an unidentified voice asks without specifying what document needed to be signed or who the signatories were, "Has there been weight loss? . . . Have they been audited?" (*O* 32).

While Harris finds anger and resentment erupting in even the conventional situation of a husband leaving for work in the morning, Claire quotes with approval a statement she attributes to Freud about the need for novelty in order to achieve orgasm. Yet it is the memory of the domestic scene of Sarah nearsightedly groping for toothpaste in the morning that most moves Harris, and Claire finds an enduring object of affection finally in the jazz pianist Sweet Papa Cream Puff who mixes nostalgic reminiscence with barefaced invention. Like the trumpet player Hokie Mokie in Barthelme's earlier "The King of Jazz," Papa Cream Puff is aware of his reputation and of the need to maintain it in the face of youthful challenge. He does so, however, not by inspired performance alone but by studying his opponent, so that he has "two or three situations on the problem" (*O* 33). Responding to the surprising possibilities that, at least in part, emerge as a comic accompaniment to Sweet Papa Cream Puff's playing as well as to the steady brilliance of his performance, Claire joyfully embraces him with sudden and unself-conscious pleasure.

In a final abrupt shift, signaled as is each of the preceding scenes by blank space, the story concludes— or almost concludes—with an insistently repeated "What?" echoing the inability to hear each other that at its start comically counterpoints the efforts of Claire and Harris to prepare dinner. The couple nonetheless achieve an optimistic if not necessarily permanent reconciliation when Harris unexpectedly makes some money in the stock market. Like Sweet Papa Cream Puff's boast of having written a piece called "Verklarte Nacht," which he explains innocently means "stormy weather," invention thus makes fun of itself. Conventionally, repeated statement establishes an exclusively linguistic and so artificial environment in which words appear unfamiliar and so strange. Here the repetition parallels the nature of the exchanges between the characters and, in fact, invites the narrative presence directly into the world they inhabit. The triumph of the everyday is startlingly confirmed by the sudden emergence of the narrator for whom, he himself admits, the act of washing the newsprint of the daily paper off his hands constitutes an affirmation of routine through which he can continue to assert his own value.

The spilling over of the framing and fictive levels of narrative into one another—a device which in one form or another Barthelme has employed in stories such

BARTHELME THE SCRIVENER

as "The Balloon," "Daumier," "Rebecca," or "On the Deck," among the more often noted examples—sends the reader outside the text to its structure for response, that is to say, directs one to the kinds of associations it establishes rather than to the narrative possibilities it invites. The illusion of an imagined world made accessible through the transparency of a narrative voice is further discredited by an unlikely reversal in which all difficulties are resolved by abrupt statement rather than by a sequence of actions consistent with what is known of the characters. It may be that this distortion of reality as much as anything else prompts Harris or the narrator—it is hard to be sure which—to urge Claire, as his last word, to smile. Yet the banal and somewhat artificial affirmation, associated with the posed awareness and fixity exhibited by the subject of a photograph, evokes an affectionate frame in which to regard those insistent if unanswerable questions that continue to provide both a challenge and a reassurance by being asked.

The triumph of ordinary interaction over the uncertainties which prevent any response to experience is confirmed by Thomas, the narrator of "The Sea of Hesitation," who abandons his efforts to change human behavior and takes instead a job processing applications for an office of the city bureaucracy called the Human Effort Administration. He has resolved insofar as possible to let people do what they want to do. Though Thomas acknowledges that "my work is, in many ways meaningless," (*O* 96), the substitution in this way of process for result, allows him to cope with the demands of his former wife that he help make life more comfortable for her and her current lover, to endure with equanimity the angry letters of a former mistress, and to listen sympathetically to the idiosyncratic interest of a current one who is absorbed in a defense of Robert E. Lee and the Confederate cause.

Like his brother Paul, who is happiest doing work other than that for which his formal training has prepared him and who has to read the daily paper in order to relieve his depression, Thomas struggles with the exaggerations of the present. At the same time, he rejects the preoccupation with the past of his friend Francesca, who is persuaded that in an earlier existence she was one of Balzac's mistresses. Even great writers, Francesca is convinced, suffer moments of doubt and concludes "The seeking after greatness is a sickness . . . It is like greed, only greed has better results" (*O* 101). Neither greatness nor greed finally prove appealing to Thomas, who rejects even truth in favor of volition and the pursuit of possibility. They are achieved, he concludes, finally only in some form of human desire and of love, which allow him to cross the Sea of Hesitation that separates him, as it does so many of Barthelme's characters, from the fulfillment possible only in the society of others. "Some people," Thomas concludes wistfully, after an idyllic description of the urgencies which mark the beginning of an affair, "have forgotten how to want" (*O* 105).

That the goal of human effort is the transient condition of love is suggested as well in "Terminus," which describes the affair between a married man and a younger woman which takes place during the unnamed couple's stay as guests in the Hotel Terminus. Despite the knowledge that the affair must end shortly and the tensions which consequently trouble even the most playful exchanges between the lovers, the joy they take in one another leads the man to behave "as if *something* were possible, still" (*O* 115). The judgment the story makes is more explictly expressed by the woman who celebrates sensuality even in the acknowledgment of its transience. "*That which exists*," she reminds him," *is more perfect than that which does not*" (*O* 116).

In the concluding story of *Overnight to Many Distant Cities*, which gives its name to the volume, the narrator assembles what appear to be a series of journal entries which provide a history of his visits to various cities around the world ranging from Stockholm to Taegu, South Korea. The entries consist of anecdotes, commentary, sometimes even accounts of meals he has eaten. In San Antonio the narrator argues for adultery as a normative activity, in Copenhagen he goes shopping with some Hungarian friends who are starved for Western material goods, in Mexico City, as a teen-ager, he runs away from home, in Berlin he is unsettled by the stares his evident happiness with a companion draws from bystanders. Occasionally the accounts are political—an Israeli journalist explains the complex politics of the Middle East, the Swedish prime minister good-naturedly accounts for the high cost of liquor in his country, the narrator is himself enlisted by a writer from an Iron Curtain country to smuggle some writing to the West.

The absence of connection as well as the relative pointlessness of the notations once again establish Barthelme's compositional principle as that of subtraction. "In London," one of the entries begins, "I met a man who was not in love" (O 171). The man's desperate insistence serves only to confirm the narrator's conviction of the value of love even as he acknowledges the frequency of his own divorces. "Show me a man who has not married a hundred times," he remarks, "and I'll show you a wretch who does not deserve the world" (O 174). Finally it is the, world or more accurately the people and events he encounters which, with or without meaning or connection, constitute the redeeming fact of existence merely by virtue of their being. Despite the unpredictability of things, underscored by weather bulletins that intermittently punctuate the central action, it is the world even with its minor imperfections (unreliable electricity in Barcelona) that leaves the narrator—and the volume itself—pleasing the Holy Ghost with his praise and in an "ecstasy of admiration for what is" they share a communal meal.

BARTHELME THE SCRIVENER

Notes

1. "Not-Knowing," *Georgia Review* 39 (Fall 1985): 522.

2. Wayne B. Stengel, *The Shape of Art in the Short Stories of Donald Barthelme* (Baton Rouge: Louisiana State UP, 1985) 161.

3. *Sixty Stories* (New York: Putnam's, 1981) 420.

4. Herman Melville, "Bartleby the Scrivener," *Selected Tales and Poems,* ed. Richard Chase (New York: Holt, 1964) 92. Further page references will be noted in parentheses.

5. The importance of rhetoric to Melville's story is perceptively examined by Sanford Pinsker, whose suggestive reading in " 'Bartleby the Scrivener': Language as Wall,"*College Literature* 2 (1975): 17–22 stands out among the unrelenting critical notice the story continues to receive. Pinsker argues that language itself constitutes a wall of rhetoric behind which the lawyer's facile optimism attempts to falsify the dark knowledge of irrationality that Bartleby's enigmatic silence refuses to blink. Though I share Pinsker's view of the importance the story places on dealing with the irrational, I find far more sympathetic Melville's treatment of the lawyer and of the limits implict in his use of language as well as his self-awareness of the comic possibilities of inflated rhetoric.

6. Quoted in *Anything Can Happen: Interviews with Contemporary American Novelists,* ed. Tom LeClair and Larry McCaffery (Urbana: University of Illinois Press, 1983) 33.

7. "Critique de la Vie Quotidienne," *Sadness* (New York: Farrar, 1972) 3–4. Further references to Barthelme's works discussed in this chapter will be given in the text and indicated by the following abbreviations: *Sadness; S; Amateurs; A; Great Days; GD; Overnight to Many Distant Cities; O.*

8. Alan Wilde, *Horizons of Assent: Modernism, Postmodernism, and the Ironic Imagination* (Baltimore: Johns Hopkins UP, 1981) 170. For the importance of the ordinary to Barthelme as a suspensive value against the hopelessness and outrage, against the sheer intractability of things, I am indebted to Wilde's indispensable study.

9. R.E.Johnson, Jr., "Bees Barking in the Night: The Beginning of Donald Barthelme's Narrative," *Boundary* 2 5 (1977): 78.

10. John M. Ditsky, " 'With Ingenuity and Hard Work, Distracted': The Narrative Style of Donald Barthelme," Style 9 (Summer 1975): 394–95.

11. J.D.O'Hara, "Donald Barthelme: The Art of Fiction LXVI" *Paris Review* 80 (1981): 197.

12. O'Hara 197.

13. O'Hara 185.

14. *Overnight to Many Distant Cities* (New York: Putnam's, 1983), 68. Further page references will be noted in parentheses.

CHAPTER FOUR

The Manifold and Dreadful Guises of Art

In Donald Barthelme's redaction of the familiar fairy tale *Snow White*, it is Walt Disney that one recognizes rather than the more primitive motifs that surface even in the literary version of the Brothers Grimm, but Walt Disney as he might have been imagined by Stephen Spielberg. Snow White is no longer the virginal idealization of co-ed charm coupled with the equally reassuring prospect of maternal self-denial, a "Janet Gaynor type" as one of Disney's early outlines described her in contrast to the Wicked Queen, who was to be "a mixture of Lady MacBeth and the Big Bad Wolf but with plenty of curves."[1] Barthelme's Snow White, tall, dark, seductively adorned by a line of beauty spots, makes love, often in the shower, to all of the seven men she lives with and writes pornographic poems while waiting for her prince to arrive. The myth from which she is drawn, like the interchangeably self-conscious characters who enact it, loses its original force and continues only as an echo in interchapters which record the memory Snow White retains of it—the memory of "the

UNDERSTANDING DONALD BARTHELME

huntsman, the forest, the steaming knife." The literary quality that results transforms instinctive desires into the determination to recapitulate established roles. The prince, for example, becomes "a prince figure," Snow White becomes conscious of her role, and the story itself, an entry in the *Oxford Companion*.

Barthelme's approach does not simply reject the usefulness of myth as a structuring device or even deliberately parody the creation of mythic parallels. In a provocative essay which relies on the paradigm established by Lévi-Strauss, John Leland traces the transformation of myth in Barthelme's fiction from cyclical to serial structure or reduplication.[2] One consequence of this shift is that Barthelme's novel lacks both the psychological interiorization which describes the fairy tale as well as the confrontation by the hero or heroine with external forces—social or natural—that constitutes myth. There is neither the enactment of the processes of growth through the symbolic confrontation between figures of innocence and experience nor the triumph of the individual over the mystery that shrouds his or her destiny. Such patterns include both the shrewdness (often self-consciously mirrored in the narrator's awareness of the circumstances through which he learns of the events) necessary in a folktale to allow the survival of a culture in a hostile environment and the value of tradition or collective wisdom in restraining vaulting individual ambition. By parodying those patterns, Barthelme's *Snow White* speaks for the environment and for the re-

THE MANIFOLD AND DREADFUL GUISES OF ART

covery of the impact it has. More central to the Barthelme version is the value of the story itself, recovering the surprise available in the linguistic vitality of popular oral forms, a vitality, the novel suggests, that had been lost through self-conscious substitution of language for either feeling or understanding and through the consequent continuing need for novelty to insure interest.

If Barthelme's novel reflects the cultural excesses that Philip Roth identified somewhat ahistorically as uniquely those which prepared for the literature of the sixties, it clearly does not reflect the subjectivity Roth found to be a consequence of that mood. It neither reveals psycho-sexual distortions at once so remote and compelling as to seem almost supernatural as in the manner of Joyce Carol Oates, nor, like the fiction of I. B. Singer, is it grounded in the oral tradition of the folktale in which magic and earthy realism are often blended. Singer, for example, frequently begins his stories by establishing their source. "The talk," he will often have a narrator begin, "turned to subjects of . . ." or, "I had just brought a cup of tea to my table when a woman I had known only slightly many years before came into the cafeteria and sitting down next to me insisted on telling of a strange event that recently befell her." Unlike these stories or those of Raymond Carver, Stephen Dixon, or Stanley Elkin, whose fiction more narrowly focuses on the dialogue, Barthelme's fiction does not create recognizable speech but a reproduction of it, one which evokes not of the way people speak but the way they sound.

Snow White's situation bears little resemblance to the fairy-tale world in which she longs to play a conventional role. At one point, in fact, in a version of the Rapunzel motif, she hopes to effect a rescue from her surroundings by letting down her hair. The gesture, whose sexuality submits itself to a series of intepretations by the other characters, suggests that literary analysis and the search for meanings within the text has itself become the subject of Barthelme's parodic focus. "There is something wrong with all those people standing there, gaping and gawking," Snow White claims, in a complaint that recalls the situation of "The Glass Mountain":

And with all those who did not come and at least *try* to climb up. To fill the role. And with the very world itself, for not being able to supply a prince. For not being able to at least be civilized enough to supply the correct ending to the story (132).

What is wrong, however, is precisely Snow White's dissatisfaction with the world or more accurately with its inescapably quotidian reality.

The actuality of Snow White's world is defined by a mixture of pedestrian, even commercial, references to brand name products (Saran Wrap, Liquid Cheer, Prell, Corfam, Mars Bars, Alka-Seltzer), to well-known

THE MANIFOLD AND DREADFUL GUISES OF ART

department stores (Bloomingdale's), nostalgically re-membered political figures (New York Mayor Fiorello LaGuardia), and somewhat esoteric religious philoso-phers (Teihard de Chardin). This pseudo-documenta-tion does not evolve out of the classic American literary mode of Hawthorne or Poe, which grounds fantastic occurrences in a supposedly historical document. Rather it isolates these individual facts from any broader context in which they might be seen to have moral sig-nificance.

Imitating various styles or aspects of reality, lan-guage comes to take on only the appearance of fact and to become invested with questionable solidity. The fa-miliar but strangely disembodied linguistic environ-ment leads to Snow White's complaint, "Oh how I wish there were some words in the world that were not the words I always hear."[3] A patient in therapy, she com-pulsively cleans house, enrolls in college courses whose catalog descriptions compress their subject matter in conveniently reductive headings, and, as one of the dwarfs complains, "sits in her room reading *Dissent* and admiring her figure in the mirror" (137).The combina-tion is strategically chosen to suggest an intellectual nar-cissism which denies the worth of the objective world and which is echoed in stream of consciousness inter-chapters in which the subjective logic of dream has little to do with the abrupt movement of thought. Accord-ingly they serve as an ironic comment on the literary technique itself as well as on the mental processes they describe. These thoughts alternate with boldface chapters consisting of mock subject headings, philosophic or historical commentary, psychological interpretation of the characters, or indications of narrative development. Each entry seems self-contained, and rather than suggesting the growth or development of character in the course of successive encounters with the world, limits itself to expressing an attitude toward them.

As Sally McNall has convincingly demonstrated, Barthelme's style is marked by the repetition of words or phrases which reflect and constantly qualify the relationships they describe between the world as subject and the world as object so that it becomes impossible to reach any conclusions.[4] The repetition, however, extends to the characters as well, who, as in a Borges story, realize—often with a sense of liberation—that everything has been done before or at least is contained within a form that holds all things simultaneously in suspension. And, like Borges, Barthelme often turns to the catalog as a limited and haphazard ennumeration that illustrates the limitlessness of objects. "The main thing that runs though my brain," Snow White complains, "is that what is, is insufficient" (135).

The dissatisfaction with reality, thus, is grounded in a dissatisfaction with the manner in which it is conceived, that is to say what is wrong is not simply with the world but with the willingness of the world to submit to the formal structure of a story. Snow White, then, does not so much long for the prince as for the "abstract notion that, to her, meant 'him'" (180). This displacement of the immediate by the ideal leads to her dissatisfaction with the bourgeois background of the prince, known simply as Paul, along with the commonness of the dwarfs, who are similarly given the ordinary names of Kevin, Edward, Hubert, Henry, Clem, Dan, and Bill, and who are interchangeable even among themselves. Echoing the restlessness the dwarfs themselves experience with normal life ("It is unbearable, this consensus, this damned felicity," one of them complains of a scene he witnesses of contented families [66]), Snow White's unhappiness extends to the ordinary occupations in which they are engaged, even against a background of peacocks who "walk through the yard in their gold suits" or what seems to be a surrealistic performance in which soldiers abandon their ordnance in order to participate in the routine of civilian life. At one point, Snow White becomes irritated by an accident which occurs while the dwarfs are cooking. "I just don't like your world," she tells them, "a world in which such things can happen" (69).

Tired of her mundane existence, Snow White resolves to change things by becoming chaste and so restoring to an ideal state what has been compromised by experience. Though she remains intrigued by the prospect of a new shower curtain intended by the dwarfs to introduce some novelty in their standard sexual practices, Snow White does manage, though by an arbitrary authorial dispensation, to become revirginized. She is not awakened at the conclusion of the novel, then, but apotheosized in a gesture that returns to the nursery-rhyme innocence of someone with skin as white as snow.

The dwarfs are similarly forced at the end to "depart in search of a new principle" and with a resigned heigh ho set about finding one as a substitute for Snow White's abstractions. Like the narrative voice, which seems distributed among them or compressed into a collective identity, the old principle is never explicitly identified. At least one possibility for it rests in the comic incongruities that go to make up contemporary American reality. Though at times they stand it on its head, the dwarfs represent, in part, that reality. Each born in a different National Park, they are self-admittedly ordinary bourgeois, who devote themselves to getting ahead and, like everyone else, prize equanimity. They wash buildings or labor over vats containing varieties of Chinese dishes, which they market in the form of baby food. Characteristically, they express themselves in non sequiturs whose staccato delivery resembles that of Groucho Marx:

The grade of pork ears we are using in the Baby Ding Sam Dew is not capable of meeting U.S. Govt. standards, or indeed, any standards. Our man in Hong Kong assures us however that the next shipment will be superior. Sales nationwide are brisk, brisk, brisk. Texas Instruments is down four points. Control Data is up four points. The pound is weakening. The cow is calving. The cactus wants watering. The new building is abuilding with leases covering 45 percent of the rentable space already in hand. The weather tomorow, fair and warmer (119–20).

Occasionally these elliptical associations operate from a principle of literalization. Stains, for example, are said to be carried in suitcases, a river of women turns into a flood that forces cars to use the sidewalks and then, as the fantasy begins to build, sends the narrator in a "felucca carrying our baggage in long canvas tubes tied, in the middle with straps." By the end of the passage, he has arrived at a village where, in an ironic treatment of yet another folk motif, the narrator challenges the signs by which the natives expect to recognize a future leader by himself proposing more traditional ones.

Like Snow White, whose presence complicates the lives of the dwarfs and confuses their struggle with her idea that "there must be something better" than the conditions in which they find themselves, Clem, one of the more articulate, complains that "most life is unextraordinary" (21). His admiration for concrete form depends on the "flowery emblemature out of the nineteenth century" which decorates the green and gold device of olive oil cans and distract him from more pressing concerns. That no one has acted upon Snow White's imaginative plan for her rescue seems to Clem painfully to underscore the ordinary quality of life in America. It reveals as well his own ambiguous feeling about it:

It suggests that Americans will not or cannot see themselves as princely . . . Of course it may be that princely is not a good thing to be. And of course there is our long democratic tradition which is anti aristocratic. Egalitarianism precludes princeliness. And yet our people are not equal in any sense. They are either . . . The poorest of them are slaves as surely as if they were chained to gigantic wooden oars. The richest of them have the faces of cold effete homosexuals. And those in the middle are wonderfully confused (141).

Paralleling Clem's unease with social structure, Henry, another of the dwarfs, expresses his dissatisfaction with the normal functioning of language. Reading sexual associations into the terms ordinarily used to describe the mechanical functions of hardware, he complains that "it is no wonder we are all going round the bend with this language dinning forever into our eyes and ears" (30). When his metaphorical interpretations lead to the accusation that he lives in a world of his own, Henry protests, "I can certainly improve on what was given" (30).

It is the resistance to what is given, however, along with the inflated heroic ambition that prompts it, which prevents action of any kind by Bill, the leader of the dwarfs, who increasingly withdraws from actuality in favor of "the ongoing circus of the mind in motion." "Give me," he pleads with his companions, "the odd linguistic trip, stutter and fall, and I will be content" (139). Grown indifferent to Snow White, Bill hopes to achieve greatness by his definitive study of anguish in Bridgeport, "city of concealed meaning," and in particular its manifestations at the university there. The search for hidden meaning is thus seen as an expression of academic criticism and its failure is given, with appropriate irony, as a result of defective scholarship. "It was," Bill complains to an unidentified but presumably professorial colleague, "because, you said, I had read the wrong book. He reversed himself in his last years, you said, in the books no one would publish. But his students remember, you said" (53).

Increasingly paranoid, Bill can no longer endure the concrete experience that comes from touching and being touched and tries to preserve his sanity by thinking about radio commercials. The strategy, however, proves unavailing, and Bill ultimately hurls two six-packs of beer at a Volkswagen whose driver had once frightened him with a "striking image." Like Snow White, Bill undergoes an apotheosis in which he rises to the heavens as a minor deity charged with presiding over the movement of dead literary forms which continually threaten to descend on an unsuspecting populace.

The artificially inflated style and mock learned rhetoric that characterize the trial at which Bill's fate is

decided give way to more colloquial expressions employed by Dan, the new leader of the dwarfs, who deals
with abstract concepts in literal terms. The production
of trash, he predicts, will soon constitute the whole of
everything. Without a sustaining alternative, his solution is to accept conditions as they are and, in fact, to
place himself "on the leading edge of this trash phenomenon" and those aspects of language that serve as
its model. Able to make the explicit connection between
the meaningless quality of experience and the breakdown of language, Dan is untroubled by the self-indulgent theorizing that prevents Bill from acting in the
world. "Analogies break down," Dan acknowledges,
"regimes break down, but the way I feel remains" (137).
What remains as well, he believes, is "work, with its
charts, its lines of authority, its air of importance" (138).

The rejection at once of contemporary reality and
literary function emerges in the inability of Paul, the
prince figure, to fulfill a definitively heroic role. Described in pedestrian terms simply as "a friend of the
family," Paul finds all courses of action equally attractive:

If I had been born well prior to 1900 [he thinks], I could
have ridden with Pershing against Pancho Villa. Alerna-
tively I could have ridden with Villa against the land-
owners and corrupt government officials of the time.
In either case, I would have had a horse. How little
opportunity there is for young men to have personally

owned horses in the bottom half of the twentieth century (78).

Paul's trivial concerns echo Snow White's resentment of the domestic role she is called upon to fulfill ("I am tired of being just a horsewife!" she complains) and at the same time are ironically mirrored in his boast of artistic self-definition. "I find it extremely interesting as a social phenomenon," Snow White tells him, "to note that during the height of what is variously called, abstract expressionism, action painting and so forth, when most artists were grouped together in a school, you have persisted in an image alone" (48). His integrity as an artist is compromised by his self-indulgence (he would rather eat exotic cuisine than rescue a beautiful princess) and by his simultaneous desire for immediate gratification and for an abstract or unworldly notion of the artist which leads him variously to experience life in a monastery in western Nevada or a post office in Rome.

Paul's unrealistic ambition proves more an expression of narcissism than heroic resolve. "Why are all these people existing under my window?" he wonders at one point, "It is as if they were as palpable as me—as bloody, as firm, as well read" (56). Like Bill, he too is unable, finally, to act decisively. "I would wish to retract everything, if I could," he admits, "so that the whole written world would be . . ." (13). Like Snow White's revirginization, the desire to retract everything parodically suggests the appeal of the abstract. Yet Paul is, significantly, unable to complete his thought. Conscious of his traditional role, he cannot imagine an alternative to the fictive existence whose demands he no longer feels capable of fulfilling. In a comic shift, the metaphor is made literal. No longer able to work at his role, Paul registers with the Unemployment Office.

Paul is on the one hand unnerved by Snow White's sexuality and on the other intimidated by ordinary responsibilities, among which he envisions dental care and piano lessons. Attempting to escape from his dilemma by a childlike retreat to his "baff," he ultimately becomes a voyeur—the inevitable fate of the artist— who avoids involvement by refusing to answer the telephone and by setting up an underground listening post where he can observe Snow White without approaching her. Overwhelmed by its imaginative forms, he mistakes art for life, and in a fittingly comic gesture that marks the overestimation of his heroic stature, he dies after drinking a poisoned vodka Gimlet intended for Snow White.

Paul and Snow White both substitute for heroism the ambition for celebrity—recognition as a result of perception rather than performance or even actual appearance—and to obtain it they self-consciously maintain a posture modeled on traditional literary expectations. When reality produces a prince uncertain of his role, Snow White regards him as a frog and concludes, "Either I have overestimated Paul, or I have overestimated history" (169). What has been overestimated, however, is the compelling power of the imagination to create a more substantial world than the one which exists.

Even the violent fantasies of the dwarfs—in part traceable to the fairy-tale source—seem stimulated as much by images, among them those drawn from the theater of cruelty, as by instinctive desires. In contrast, a more unconstrained expession of earthy lust is demonstrated by Hogo de Bergerac and his companion, Jane, who parallels the wicked stepmother of the original version. Callous enough to be a match even for the Internal Revenue Service, Hogo takes delight in the atrocities of his heritage and manages to inspire the dwarfs both by his thought and language. In contrast to the calculated utterances of Snow White and her prince, Hogo boasts of his random vileness "not only because it is expected of me but also because I enjoy it" (73). A mixture of affected foreign locutions, mock patriotic sentiment, psychological jargon, and exaggerated metaphor which concludes with the injunction to "remember what Freud said," without otherwise identifying the particular quotation to which he alludes, Hogo's male chauvinist speech affirms the value of popular "cheap" music, fast foods, and the sensual if transient beauty of women. Like the tastelessness of his house, whose ceiling is decorated with General Motors advertisements and whose walls consist of chain-link fencing, Hogo's appeal to vulgarity evokes such echoes of postmodernism as Robert Venturi's defense of the architectural gaudiness of Las Vegas. "My main point," Hogo tells the dwarfs, "is that you should bear in mind multiplicity and forget about uniqueness" (75). Though considered vile, Hogo brings a refreshing coarseness to the vapid gentility around him; however his vitality cannot overcome Snow White's romantic longings and when he confesses his love for her he is rejected because of his lack of noble blood.

Unlike Snow White's insistence on tradition, Hogo is willing to accept the compromised conditions of reality—including aging and death—comically confirmed in his habit of dumping garbage from his window. The action both literalizes and serves as a paradigm of the popular aspects of culture the dwarfs designate as trash. Philip Stevick has recognized in the inclusion of such dreck in our fiction a way of acknowledging the common bonds of our lives and of investing its transitory quality with a comic specificity that makes it bearable.[5] By making marginal objects important, Barthelme corrects as well the skewed values that have attached alternately to both the dominant social or institutional aspects of culture and to those of individualism which has opposed them. Simply by naming objects—an artificial strategy of statement rather than an organic process of development—he allows them to confer a solidity of recognizable presence. It is, perhaps, this impulse that accounts for the judgment made by an unnamed dwarf who prefers the jacket copy of a book to its content:

THE MANIFOLD AND DREADFUL GUISES OF ART

We like books that have a lot of *dreck* in them, matter which presents itself as not wholly relevant (or indeed, at all relevant) but which, carefully attended to, can supply a kind of "sense" of what is going on. This "sense" is not to be obtained by reading between the lines (for there is nothing there, in those white spaces) but by reading the lines themselves—looking at them and so arriving at a feeling not of satisfaction exactly, that is too much to expect, but of having read them, of having "completed" them (106).

The idea of accepting the superficial value of an object rather than pressing for a more meaningful or symbolic examination is underscored in Jane's resistance to her mother's attempt to interpret Hogo's actions. Her wickedness, however, is initially expressed as a function of her approach to art. Complementing Hogo's random manner, Jane arbitrarily selects a name from the phone book, a Mr. Quistgaard, in order to reclaim the power formerly conferred by her physical beauty by entering what she terms his "universe of discourse" (44). The phrase carries into the subjective attempt to unify thought and feeling that stands at the center of modernism, a more contemporary awareness that such exchanges occur only within the inherent textual ambiguities and conflicting interpretations that separate the experience of the writer from that of her audience. The intrusion of Jane's discourse into the concrete immediacy of Quistgaard's comfortable American life suggests an energizing force for self-examination. At the same time, it dilutes the concrete particularity in which Quistgaard exists and thus seems somehow sinister as well as liberating. Barthelme does not indicate Quistgaard's response, but the reaction to the threatening quality of such an intellectual challenge can be inferred from a dream in which the dwarfs substitute Snow White for the heroine of Carl Dreyer's film, which they punningly recall as "The Burning of Joan of Art."

The ambivalent nature of a literary past is suggested as well by allusions to fictive sources Barthelme continues to inject throughout the novel, ranging from reference to James Baldwin ("The Fire Next Time Bar & Grille") to ironic allusions to Henry Adams and Malcolm Lowry. The challenge to conventional ideas of fictional form, however, is more strikingly apparent in the much-commented upon questionnaire with which Barthelme concludes part 1 of the three sections into which the novel is divided. It consists of such questions as, "Do you like the story so far?" "Are the seven men, in your view, adequately characterized as individuals?" "Has the work for you, a metaphysical dimension?" Each of the questions is followed by a blank space enclosed by parentheses, in which the reader is invited to check off a response. The playful self-consciousness of the device parodies not only the unrelieved gravity which frequently attends the writing of fiction but also the school assignment approach that colors criticism of it. More importantly, like Jane's letter to Mr. Quistgaard, it intrudes on the reader, compelling an awareness of a world outside that circumscribed within the fictive imagination.

In like manner, the divisions of the novel themselves exaggerate the absence of fluid transitions rather than satisfy the formal demands of narrative development. Part 2, for example, begins with the dwarfs' uncertainty whether to alter the routine of their lives, part 3 with Snow White's resolve to maintain an "esthetic" distance from her former lovers. The routine of behavior and the detachment from it afforded, even necessitated, by art are surely among the central themes which continue to surface throughout the novel. But though Snow White's decision is framed in temporal terms—"From now on," she decides, "I deny myself to them" (135)—the divisions do not signal a significant movement in time or space that prepares for what is to come or indicate a periodicity and so provisional finality of what has already happened. Discontinuous rather than sequential, decorative rather than organic, the same set of conditions is made to occur again and again, so that even seeming digressions become part of an overall pattern. The denial of progressive development frustrates the expectation of serial form as well as of narrative content. Events appear to take place all at once, ending without completion. The imbalance proposed at the beginning of the novel, accordingly, is resolved only by proposing yet another set of recognizable but partial forms, similarly unrelated, so that everything that happens is collapsed into a single plane.

The rejection of depth is nowhere more pronounced than in the several references throughout the novel to Henry James, whose essays no less than his fiction continue to stand as a landmark of the moral seriousness and psychological truths to which art aspires in contrast to a commercial society and the vulgar pieties behind which it conceals its crassness. In his seminal "The Art of Fiction," James advanced the analogy between the art of the novelist and that of the painter. Though he militantly opposed any restrictions on the form which either chooses to represent reality, he argued strongly for the seriousness with which the artist must resist any concessive acknowledgment of its own condition. In its broadest sense, he claimed, a novel was "a personal, direct impression of life." This subjective identification of the artist with the art, of the art with the way things appear to the artist, led James to describe the novel as similarly resistant to an objective set of rules or conditions. Rejecting the notion of the novel as a "series of blocks," he insisted, above all, on its unity. "A novel," he claimed, "is a living thing, all one and continuous, like any other organism, and in proportion as it lives will it be found, I think, that in each of the parts there is something of each of the other parts."[6]

It is exactly this organic view that is rejected in *Snow*

THE MANIFOLD AND DREADFUL GUISES OF ART

White. John Carlos Rowe calls attention to a collage Barthelme made by pasting colored strips of paper across a photograph of James to give him the appearance of wearing an Indian headdress. Barthelme called the work "Henry James, Chief," and by it, Rowe argues, he meant to suggest the connection between his own "comedy of unexpected juxtapositions" and the art of one of the founding fathers of modernism, an art which "demonstrates how every form, meaning, or concept is determined by a language that cannot succeed in delivering its message or truth."[7] In his examination of the complexity of social relations, James surely alternated between a sense of the necessity of such discriminations in giving value to experience and the corresponding inability ever fully to know or even understand its subtleties or ambiguities. But for James, as for the modernists who followed and were influenced by him, the "atmosphere of the mind," as he called it, was breathable as successive layers. The higher one went, the more rarified the air of reality, the more painful and heroic the attempt to exist. Barthelme, in contrast, resists the neatness of such an equation between truth and the peeling away of surfaces. When, in fact, Paul presents Snow White with a "new thing" he has created, it proves to be a "dirty great banality in white, off-white and poor-white, leaned up against the wall," which despite its poor quality, or rather because of it, Paul is prepared to hurl into the marketplace (48). The willingness to submit, if not to the judgment at least to the activity of the marketplace, rather than remain confined by traditional symbols of authority is reinforced in a description of the occupation in which the dwarfs are engaged: the manufacture their own brand of Chinese baby food, whose recipe, they acknowledge, came from their father:

"Try to be a man about whom nothing is known," our father said, when we were young. Our father said several other interesting things, but we have forgotten what they were. "Keep quiet," he said. That we remember. He wanted more quiet. One tends to want that in a National Park. Our father was a man about whom nothing was known. Nothing is known about him still. He gave us recipes. He was not very interesting. A tree is more interesting. A suitcase is more interesting. A canned good is more interesting. When we sing the father hymn, we notice that he was not very interesting. The words of the hymn notice it. It is explicitly commented upon, in the text (18–19).

The source of Barthelme's parody is Henry James's famous admonition that the writer go beyond what is immediately present in his experience to trace the implications of things. "Try to be one of those people on whom nothing is lost!" is what James urged, in addition to affirming the obligation to make the novel interesting.[8] About what constituted interest, James was deliberately vague. About its source, he was much more explicit. It was located in proportion to the revelation of "a particular mind" and attributed to the intensity of

THE MANIFOLD AND DREADFUL GUISES OF ART

the writer's impressions of life. What Barthelme parodies, then, is just those impressions or, more accurately,
the efforts of an inquiring intelligence to substitute the
significance they yield for the more objective reality
from which they are drawn. "Everyone wanders around
having his own individual perceptions," Kevin, another
of the dwarfs complains in yet another parodic reference to one of James's notable stories, "These, like balls
of different colors and shapes and sizes, roll around on
the green billiard table of consciousness . . . Where is
the figure in the carpet? Or is it just . . . carpet?" (129).

The breathless struggle to be interesting, in fact,
accounts largely for the restlessness experienced by the
dwarfs, one of whom wonders if they should not be
doing something less ordinary with their lives. "One
tends the vats," he thinks, "and carries the money to
the vault and never stops for a moment to consider that
the whole process may be despicable" (87). On the other
hand, Barthleme suggests, it may not, or at least not
entirely. This ironic assessment of the value of equanimity is balanced by Paul's equally ironic boast that if more
withdrawn than his father, the king, he is also more
experimental. Nonetheless, he must acknowledge even
in his father's frivolous behavior an inherent nobility,
whose most enduring monument was "the de-deifica-
tion of his own person":

He was peculiar, my father. That much can be safely
said. He knew some things that other men do not know.

He heard the swans singing just before his death, and
the bees barking in the night. That is what he said, but
I didn't believe him, then. Now I don't know" (28).

At once evocative and prosaic, the unlikely combinations of singing swans and barking bees invest an
otherwise discredited authority with some troubling in-
timations of conviction. Barthelme makes sure the point
is not missed by devoting an entire interchapter to the
boldfaced message, "Anathematization of the world is
not an adequate response to the world" (178). Just what
is an adequate response is less clear. If it is to be arrived
at at all, it will be both through and despite language,
whose distortions, as the dwarf Henry advises one of
his colleagues, combine both the ecstasy and misery
that follow the attempt to uproot the past. Explaining
to the dwarfs why she remains with them, Snow White
confesses that she has not been able to imagine anything better. This ironic admission has often been read
as a literal confirmation of Snow White's failure of
imagination. In fact, however, as the dwarfs understand, it confirms "our essential mutuality, which can
never be sundered or torn, or broken apart, dissipated,
diluted, corrupted or finally severed, not even by art in
its manifold and dreadful guises" (59).

In *The Dead Father*, the rejection of the past comes
about through a journey no one is anxious to make and

THE MANIFOLD AND DREADFUL GUISES OF ART

which will leave matters in much the same condition as when they began. Barthelme thus reduces the conflict from one of heroic enactment to that of repetitive statement, allowing neither, as in comedy, the triumphant celebration of youth over age nor, as in tragedy, the transcendence of necessity through understanding. Nurturing and destructive, omnipotent and ineffectual, tyrannical as well as bewildered, vulnerable no less than vindictive, the Dead Father is a figure of undiminished sexual appetites and vague unfulfilled longings, whose farcical attempt to perpetuate his own myth invites an ambivalent response. Almost from the start, it undercuts its own resonance by substituting for the ritual gesture or expression an uncertain questioning about how effectual such gestures or expressions have been.

The novel begins with the Dead Father, in a sense already dead though not interred; that is, he has outlived the period of his greatest potency. Yet even as he is taken from the city by his son, Thomas, Thomas's lover, Julie, and 19 of the Dead Father's other children, and hauled across an undefined landscape for burial, the Dead Father remains alert and even—his eyes are wide open—all seeing. The combination of helplessness and arbitrary exercise of power is recapitulated in the father's childlike demand to be told a story that betrays his own apprehension and longing for protection. The story is told by Thomas, who confirms in it both his own fears of inadequacy and the sense of parental ferocity and omnipotence. Thomas tells of being kidnapped and

taken far from the city, whose complexity is thus identified with youth and security, even with innocence. In
contrast, the wild country across which he is forced to
travel is pictured as more primitive or instinctual. The
kidnappers are four men whose shirts, ties, submachine
guns, and attaché cases testify to their authority. Without specifying the matter at issue, they tell Thomas he
was "wrong and had always been wrong and would
always be wrong."[9] While, like all adults, assuring him
that he will not be hurt, the kidnappers proceed to beat
him with can openers, documents, and harsh words.
After an arduous journey clearly emblematic of the process of maturity, Thomas is confronted by a sphinxlike
"Father Serpent," whose riddle he must solve. "What
do you really feel?" Thomas is challenged. His answer,
"Like murderinging," comes with its own internal echo,
at once festive and insistent, and is learned by reading
a mirror image of the father's own words. Over the
Dead Father's protest, Thomas defensively adds a gloss
not only of his own tall tale but of the novel as well.
"No tale ever happened in the way we tell it," he contends, "but the moral is always correct" (46).

Subsequently, Thomas is able to obtain, one by
one, the symbols of the father's authority—his belt
buckle, sword, passport, keys—until, at length, though
still with great reluctance, the Dead Father consents to
his own burial. Despite this successful performance of
ritual and though neither Julie nor Emma (an alternately
seductive presence on the journey), responds to the

THE MANIFOLD AND DREADFUL GUISES OF ART

Dead Father's sexual overtures, Thomas remains unable to take his father's place. "A son," he is assured, "can never, in the fullest sense become a father" (33). Though the Dead Father subsequently softens this judgment, he continues to maintain a condescending attitude toward his son. "Some amount of amateur effort is possible," he admits.

Speaking in a variety of dialects and voices described variously as sounding like burning film, marble being quarried, or "the clash of paper clips by night" (122), the Dead Father combines the truly abrasive, even grotesque, with a comically reductive self-imitation that often disguises an oppressive presence behind a folksy manner. Even in death, then, the father remains both arbitrary and omnipotent, devouring his children—improperly laundered blue jeans, Thom McAns and all—and imposing his imperatives through an inner voice "commanding, harranguing, yessing and no-ing, a binary code yes no yes no yes no yes no, governing [their] slightest movement, mental or physical" (144).

Along with the wholesale and indiscriminate slayings that follow his infrequent sexual frustration, the Dead Father's exaggerated boasts of his mythical virility serve at once to demonstrate and mock his procreative force. Something of this feeling is suggested in a list of things he boasts of having fathered, which betrays a nostalgic fondness for often useless and frequently outdated objects. These include:

The poker chip, the cash register, the juice extractor, the kazoo, the rubber pretzel, the cuckoo clock, the key chain, the dime bank, the pantograph, the bubble pipe, the punching bag both light and heavy, the inkblot, the nose drop, the midget Bible, the slot-machine slug, and many other useful and human cultural artifacts, as well as some thousands of children of the ordinary sort (36).

There is no attempt to connect these disparate objects, and it is, in fact, the implict notion of a unifying principle that Barthelme seems to be mocking most of all. The sheer number of objects alone tends to make them comic, existing for their own sake rather than contributing to the development of the plot or even of the character. The reductive jokiness correspondingly diminishes the stature of the Dead Father. His tall tale grows increasingly wilder, ending in an anticlimactic pool game and a spectacular phallic triumph in which it is the exaggeration of myth finally that is made fun of. At the same time, the narrative seems to share the Dead Father's unmistakable exhuberance, even sheer joy in the ennumeration of these objects, not because they help us to understand or even structure the environment of which they are a part, but because they testify to its continuing existence.

The point is explicitly made in several exchanges between Julie and Emma, which discontinuously alternate voices of cultural sophistication. The two women exchange insults, threats, and, in what seem to be the fragments of overheard conversation, the clichés with which formal occasions are frequently punctuated. Not paying attention or perhaps unable to credit what is being said, one or the other—the absence of attributive dialogue tags make it unclear at times who is speaking, the point being it doesn't matter—asks repeatedly to have things repeated. "Repetition," the first voice finally concedes, "is reality" (87).

Struck by the somewhat similar thought that the purpose of his dealings with the Dead Father may serve as a rehearsal for his own career, Thomas acknowledges the complex interweaving of events that have little centripetal force:

Things are not simple. Error is always possible, even with the best intentions in the world. People make mistakes. Things are not done right. Right things are not done. There are cases which are not clear. You must be able to tolerate the anxiety. To do otherwise is to jump ship, ethics-wise (93).

Despite the glib contemporaneity of the conclusory moral, the need to tolerate anxiety here, as in Barthelme's fiction in general, carries a good deal of conviction, even poignance. Yet the acceptance of uncertainty it proposes is not, finally, by itself enough. The only child of marriage, or marriages, which Thomas describes as a movement from comedy to farce to burlesque, his anxiety more properly is lodged in the inability to imagine himself as capable of duplicating an adequate response to the past and to the father in whom its authority is invested. The attempt to do so leads Thomas to describe himself as a student of decay and when his father complains that like all young men he never understood the larger picture, he can only echo Hogo's assertion in *Snow White* that he has instead been aware of its limiting frame. The repetition that establishes reality is thus reduced to an intermittent stutter. For the Dead Father, on the other hand, the question of whether he is faced with a copy or an original produces only a "cool anxiety about whether [he] had been cogged if if if with a restrike or not," a concern far less troubling than "the action of the sun fading what I valued most, strong browns turning to pale browns if not vacant yellows" (18). Projected in visual blocks, what the Dead Father fears, in short, is the erosion of time on his issue, literary no less than biological.

Only when they encounter the Wends, a tribe which fulfills the oedipal desire to marry their own mothers, does Thomas see the possibility of evading the awful power of the Dead Father. Principally valued for their sexuality, women are unable to provide the stability afforded by the father but, as Julie complains, constitute an overall presence more like grime (77). Relentless in pursuit as she is mysterious in identity, the menacing figure of woman is revealed as the mother who has grimly continued to follow the party on horseback throughout their journey, thus adding yet another level

THE MANIFOLD AND DREADFUL GUISES OF ART

of meaning to the term "horsewife." When her identity becomes known, the Dead Father can barely remember her name, and she is charged with the one responsibility for which society has come to depend on her: she is asked to do the shopping. The joke which has the entire novel for its buildup is echoed by the complementary stereotype provided by Julie, who tracks her male suitors with a loaded harpoon gun and willingly ignores sense data in making the world over into the image she wishes to have of it. In contrast to Thomas, whom she accuses of reveling in a sense of injury, she lets nothing interfere with her schemes, even if that means she must go against reality. "I put out of my mind that which is injurious to mind," she explains and, hoping to substitute the sexuality of personal relationships for the erosions of time, invites Thomas to think of them as "the two of us against the is" (68).

Though Thomas readily welcomes the distraction of sex, he is unwilling to abandon the notion of an absolute principle, even when, paradoxically, it presents itself as mutability. At the same time as he questions his ability to assume an independent identity, he is intimidated by the inexorable processes which, at least viewed from above, lead even the Dead Father in a straight line to death. Accordingly Thomas recognizes "fatherhood as a substructure of the war of all against all" (76).

The complex nature of his struggle both with and for fatherhood is examined in a largely self-contained section of the novel designated "A Manual for Sons." The manual is advertised as a translation from English into English, and the repetition not only alludes to the difficulties language places in the way of understanding or even verifiability. It calls attention as well to the problematic relation between a copy and the original, which is to say, reality. In fact, the 23 sections into which it is divided mirror the number of chapters of the novel proper in which it is embedded. Each of these sections is illuminated by a mock-medieval woodcut. The figures depicted have little bearing on the specific content and rather than illustrate what is being said merely parody its overall homiletic tone. The burden of the manual is summed up in its concluding section, which absolves the son of the necessity to actively displace the father. That action, it maintains, can confidently be left to time. Rather than struggle for an independent identity, then, which in any case is unattainable, the son is admonished to imitate the father though "in attenuated form . . . thus moving toward a golden age of decency, quiet, and calmed fevers" (145). The prospect of fatherhood is so intimidating that any attempt to make it seem less so can come only at the expense of a lowered sense of one's own self-worth. " 'Small' is what you should shoot for," the son is advised, and though an ambiguous irony qualifies the further encouragement he is given to perform a series of exercises which will confirm the idea of his limited competence, somewhat more reassuring is the notion that in this way *fatherhood can be,*

THE MANIFOLD AND DREADFUL GUISES OF ART

if not conquered, at least 'turned down' in this generation"
(145).

Not surprisingly, it is an effort which the Dead
Father rejects. Only with reluctance does he accede to
the natural order, and envisions himself as an artist
whose aesthetic interest has been sacrificed to the need
for production and whose influence is inescapable. "All
lines my lines," he boasts. "All figure and all ground
mine, out of my head. All colors mine" (19). Self-pitying
about his advancing age, he is nonetheless unwilling to
surrender any of his prerogatives. His vulnerability,
however, is suggested by the reductive even ludicrous
appearance he continues to make. His vaunted sexual
drive must be sublimated in reading pornographic
comic books. Allowed to make a speech, what comes
out is a mixture of sociological, scientific, religious, and
philosphical double-talk. Ultimately his death goes un-
remarked even by a monument, and the novel ends
with the single terse word, "Bulldozers," an allusion at
once to the Dead Father's power and to its transience.

The fragility which informs the Dead Father's
seeming omnipotence is revealed in Julie's recognition
that "he is like a bubble that you do not wish to burst,"
and it is ultimately acknowledged in his own admission
that he had all along been aware of the funereal nature
of the journey. "I wasn't really fooled," he tells Thomas.
"Not for a moment. I knew all along" (176). If the journey has a direction, it does not have progressive development. When the children are asked what they will

do afterward, they, too, admit they have no answer, either in terms of what can be imagined or the reality they have experienced.

The static quality of the narrative style in *The Dead Father* is characterized by the use of noun phrases and nonfinite verbs or by the elimination of predicates so that like Barthelme's fiction in general the linguistic elements turn actions into objects which do not yield their meaning through the formal development of beginning, middle, and end. This elliptical technique, which amounts really to objectification without representation and accounts for much of the opacity in Barthelme's fiction, occurs in perhaps its most bewildering form halfway through the journey when the burial procession stops to rest near a cathedral while a religious service is in progress. The scene is described:

The mountain. The cathedral. The stone steps. Music. Looking down. The windows, apertures. Rows of seated people. The altars, lights, singing. Egg-shaped apertures like seats opening onto the void. The drop. The clouds. Slipping in the seat. Thomas slipping in the seat. Toward the void. Brace foot against edge (84).

Outside the cathedral, the Dead Father sits in a garden with Julie, who is sketching. The two actions—Thomas slipping into the void, Julie sketching the scene—are juxtaposed as part of what can be read alternately as a combined erotic and religious experience or as the directions given in an instructional manual. The antecedent reference implied by the repeated use of the definite article is never made explicit and, in fact, the listing of elements makes sense only when it is seen as anticipating some event rather than looking back to one. The paragraph ends: "Slipping. Sketching. Slipping," and the terms establish a pictorial tension between the human activity and the attempt in art to arrest its temporal movement, an attempt itself subject to that process of decay.

Such pictorial awareness, which must be seen as distinct from visualization, is integral to Barthelme's technique. When the Dead Father protests that a tractor would have been more appropriate than the 19 men actually used to haul the cable by which he is dragged across the countryside, he is told, "The composition would have suffered." The discontinuity of the elements suggests that the narrative principle is more onomastic, or naming, than visual. Neither the objects named nor the relationships between them are arranged in any necessary order by combining the parts to afford some perspective or by widening the view of landscape. Nor is order determined by the evolving character of one or another of the actors as a consequence of what happens to them. They are, rather, allowed simply to remain side by side. In Barthleme's fiction, then, juxtaposition proves to be regressive rather than developmental. The Dead Father's acquiescence in his burial punctuates the loss of the symbols of his authority; it is not caused by that loss or even illuminated by it.

Nonetheless the influence of traditional forms cannot be escaped. The Dead Father, the reader discovers, is "dead but still with us, still with us but dead" (3) and so forces upon his progeny a legacy inapplicable to the world as it presently exists but equally impossible to disavow. Though the narrative neither evokes nor approximates the texture of reality nor attempts to enter the consciousness of the characters and so arrive at the essence of things, the Dead Father insists on having it both ways. In a Joycean soliloquy which immediately precedes his burial, he both rails against and celebrates the incompleteness of things:

AndI. EndI. Great endifarce teeterteeterteetertottering . . . And having made them, where now? what now? . . . AndI understand but list, list, let's go back. To the wetbedding. To the dampdream. AndI a oneohsevenyearoldboy, just like the rest of them. Pitterpatter. I reiterate&reiterate&reiterate&reiterate, pitterpatter (171).

The punning allusion to the catalog ("but list, list") and the self-pitying (pity pater) perhaps onomatopoeic echo of a heartbeat give way finally to the Dead Father's poignant appeal, "Pitterpatter Oh please pitterpatter," which suggests his hope to defer a while longer the

THE MANIFOLD AND DREADFUL GUISES OF ART

anonymous call for bulldozers that announces his immi-
nent burial. Like the judgment made of his resonant
voice by his son Thomas, the Dead Father's struggle
both to generate and to possess the world and to recon-
stitute it as a legacy has been both intolerable and
grand. For Barthleme, the literary prospects, at least,
are equally inventive, equally referential. Content with
neither the modernist attempt to evade or to structure
the chaotic world nor with the postmodern joyful immersion in it, he hopes, in a repetitive rather than developmental framework, to obtain at least a brief reprieve.

A similar reprieve from the process of aging is almost magically granted to Simon, the 53-year-old central figure of *Paradise*, Barthelme's most recent novel,
when, one afternoon he meets three young women
modeling lingerie in a bar on Lexington Avenue. A successful Philadelphia architect, Simon had come to New
York for a sabbatical when he discovered a pipe bomb
left underneath his car by a disgruntled contractor. A
more compelling reason, he admits, is his dissatisfaction with his marriage, and when he learns the models
have no money and are temporarily without a place to
live he invites them to share an apartment he has sublet
for a year. The unlikely situation is thus grounded in
recognizably commonplace terms, which, although they
have all the elements of an erotic male fantasy, prove
instead an orgy of domesticity. Even explicit sexual encounters are described with a casual indifference to the

urges which appear to prompt them. "We talked a lot," is the way Simon recalls his experience with the women, "I think of it as a series of conversations. A series of ordinary conversations. Simple as pie."[10]

The ordinary, of course, proves a good deal more complex. Simon recognizes the contrasting aspects of the contemporary sensibility in the opposition between the desire for light and the need for safety. One impulse, he realizes, results in the construction of increasingly tall buildings, the other leads to living in caves. Simon additionally projects this conflict in the contrast between the "messianic-maniacal idea that architecture will make people better, civilize them" that informed the International Style and a more decorative contemporary architecture, which he thinks of as a cottage industry whose excesses remind him of graffiti or of the playful exaggerations of a circus (68–69). Accordingly, he prefers the mock-heroic architectural style of Michael Graves or the complexity and contradiction that Robert Venturi gives his buildings to the classical form-givers "Michelangelo, Wright and his cape, Mies and his pinstripes" (80).

Simon's rebellion against form is not so much a reaction against the past as an attempt to prevent his estrangement from the present. He is, the women continually remind him and each other, twice as old as they are. He is incredulous when he learns that they never heard of the Marshall Plan and wonders about the reference on a T-shirt that reads "Ally Sheedy lives." The

THE MANIFOLD AND DREADFUL GUISES OF ART

joke, of course, rests as much with the contrast of Simon's sober response to so preeminently contemporary a phenomenon as the message on a T-shirt as it does with the implied critique of the movie actress named on it.

But while popular culture makes fun, in this way, of its own forms, Simon attempts to establish a more enduring scale of values. To do so he looks to the artificiality of his collection of radios or to lists of jazz musicians that reflect a history of transmitted influence. Objecting to the views of one of his teachers that there are no right angles in nature, he points to the abrupt shifts signaled in the cornstalk, the departure of friends, the telephone pole, and in political assassinations. Nature, in short, confronts humanity with losses for which it is unprepared. At one point, in fact, Simon almost crushes his hand getting a refrigerator down a set of right-angled stairs. The women, too, he is aware, will soon leave. "Their movement through the world," he reflects, "required young men, a class to which he did not belong," and with whom, Simon ruefully acknowledges, they make love "in joyous disregard of history, economics, building codes" (178). Aware of all three, Simon, in a gesture that combines anger, resentment, and generosity, constructs an egg out of which hatch three naked young men, each of whom, he imagines, is named Harry and so is indistinguishable from the others. Simon's action in tempting his multiple Eves with an egg rather than, say, an apple is illuminating in several ways. To begin with, it is, of course, the punchline to a joke. A white plaster egg, eight feet tall is positioned like a minimal sculpture in the middle of a New York apartment not to generate an esthetic solution to the restlessness of the women who live there but as an expression of the artist's anxiety. In a reversal of roles, the women do not hatch the egg, Simon shatters it with an iron-headed maul. But perhaps most significantly, the egg does not precipitate the women's expulsion from Paradise; it signals their desire to leave. The episode thus reveals the fear of advancing age Simon has thus far attempted to deny and the reaction he feels women have to it and to men in general. Women, he acknowledges at one point, are like anthills "splendid, stinging anthills" (30). Consequently he understands why, since all sculpture is ultimately about women, even the artist Alberto Giacometti, who deals with them in wiry abstractions, carries a razor in his shoe.

Narrated in the present, the passages dealing with the models present Simon with the reality of things in the face of constantly changing conditions. Their verbal exchanges in particular, edged and immediate, are at once knowing and repetitive. Above all, perhaps, they are invested with many of the same anxieties that trouble Simon. Noting the high ceilings of the apartment one of them observes, "You could hang yourself in here" (13). Subsequently, unable to find work other than modeling at an industrial convention, she complains, "We are pure skin" (143). Although the women

THE MANIFOLD AND DREADFUL GUISES OF ART

fantasize about entering Juilliard or medical school, they are aware that pragmatically the only careers open to them are marriage or waitressing and even formal education, as one of them tells Simon, would leave them as dreary when they completed it as when they began.

Simon is, in fact, forced to acknowledge that education has for the most part been unable to prevent such self-destructive acts as the United States involvment in Vietnam, yet he cannot accept the irresponsible alternative presented by Tim, whom one of the women meets in a laundromat and whose counter-cultural protest is perhaps best suggested by his becoming a professional whistler. A graduate of Cornell in electrical engineering, Tim earns his living by working at a car wash, which he leaves to start a law firm specializing in malpractice suits. Like the models, he is at once childlike and knowledgeable. Influenced by Buckminister Fuller, he is convinced of vast governmental and industrial conspiracies, whose existence he supports with nebulous statistics delivered in a rapid-fire speech marked by clichés drawn from computer jargon. Dressed in a $700 Paul Stuart suit, he invites the models to lunch at a fast-food restaurant, explaining, "Our cash flow is not on line as yet" (160). At least as revealing is his response to the reassurance by one of the women that his situation is only temporary. "By me," Tim replies, "everything's temporary. Good things and bad things." Though seemingly ironic, this deadpan echo of the further judgment that such indeterminacy must be fascinating carries no more indication—linguistic, syntactic, situational, tonal—of how it should be taken than did the original comment.

A parallel uncertainty clouds the outcome of a brief affair Simon has—he describes it as a detour—with a red-headed poet he meets, appropriately, at a fast-food restaurant. Like that of the models, part of the poet's appeal is her childlike innocence. When he comes to visit, she greets Simon sitting on the hood of her pick-up truck, drinking apple juice out of a paper cup and playfully changing the words of the nursery song to "Row Row Row your bed / Gently down the stream." Though only ten years younger than Simon, she annoys him with the nickname "Pappy." Her resistance to allowing the affair to develop beyond playfulness seems shaped by her feeling that her parents have been unable to reconcile the personality differences in their marriage. Her mother has given her a Biedermier chair, her father an Eames chair in the shape of a potato chip. "That tell you anything?" she asks Simon (145). Her poetry tells him at least as much. Marked by recurrent images of dust and burning barns, it reveals an awareness of mortality that she, like Simon, has difficulty confronting directly. "My dust," she replies when Simon questions her about the images that appear in her poetry, "My excellent dust. You're a layman, Simon, shut up about my dust" (157).

Fires throughout the novel are, however, equally associated with the contrasting ideas of youthfulness

THE MANIFOLD AND DREADFUL GUISES OF ART

and innocence. As a child, Simon's daughter, Sarah, would put a battery in his ear, prompting him to make a sound like a fire engine or sitting in a fire truck he bought her "put out many exciting fires with it" (36). Accompanied by the models, Simon himself goes on occasion to the A & P at an hour when they knew the firemen from a local firehouse would do their shopping. "The firemen were good-looking, Simon noticed, appeared strong and trustworthy and very decent. He wondered about the fireman-population, where all this decency and goodness came from" (35). More to the point, however, is where it goes to. Though the models assure Simon they are not interested in the firemen, when Veronica has a brief affair with one of them, he turns out to be married.

Beneath innocence, then, can be found the deceits of mortality. Simon's relations with his daughter are confined exclusively to telephone conversations, in one of which he learns that she had become pregnant and spontaneously aborted. The poet, too, reveals something of the compromised conditions of existence and of the difficulty in dealing with it. Describing her midwestern background and the naïvete often associated with it, she tells Simon of the consequent insecurity it occasions: "If you're not from Kansas, people in Kansas ask you: What do you think about Kansas? What do you think about our sky? What do you think about people in Kansas. Are we dumb? . . . You find a high degree of sadness in Kansas" (157).

UNDERSTANDING DONALD BARTHELME

Simon experiences that sadness at the death of his father, whom he remembers with fondness as a large, calm, and, at 75, still-active man "playing the market and raising hell on behalf of the ADA" (111). Despite a successful business career which did not interfere with his idealistic belief in the values for which the Second World War was fought, the father appears in Simon's dreams as both inadequate and uncaring. He is seemingly without friends—apart from Simon and his mother, the funeral is attended only by an elderly couple who formed part of a golfing foursome in which his father played—and even in Simon's dreams he is indifferent to his father's accomplishments until shamed into paying attention. Though he approves of and admires his father, Simon's own beliefs are centered more concretely in the practical world he characterizes by bricks and bricklayers. Nonetheless he claims to have a "tragic sense of brick" and is aware that "even bricklayers get things wrong" (202).

Simon's anxieties present themselves in a succession of nightmares which reveal a sense both of inadequacy and guilt. In one of these dreams, he is forced to serve the inmates of a leper colony and so finds himself an outcast even among outcasts. In another his wife, Carol, drives a bus full of people into the front of his office building, distracted, she explains, by a passenger who insisted that she change a fifty-dollar bill into nine fives. The obvious symbolism of nine to five or the frustrations of the ordinary workday are here underscored by Simon's awareness that his wife is being short-changed. In yet another dream, Simon finds himself at once constricted by a gray, pin-striped jacket, and unprepared as he struggles against the clock to deliver a talk he is scheduled to make over television. Simon's difficulty with time and with the responsibilities it confronts him with extend as well to the image he has of his own potency. Though he is able to satisfy all three women, one of whom boasts of the number of orgasms she is able to achieve with him, he is compelled to silently endure a discussion of his inadequacies, one of which, he later feels, may be their impression that he is not even a father-figure but "more like a guy who's stayed out in the rain too long" (112).

Simon's sense of sexual inadequacy, however, is not grounded solely in an oedipal notion of the family romance but in a general conviction about the infidelity of women, which he ties to a seemingly irrelevant childhood betrayal. Asked by the models about his first sexual experience, he recalls an incident in which a teacher admired his school project but subsequently discarded it when another boy submitted one she judged to be better. What is significant, of course, is Simon's understanding of the incident as sexual. Not even women (or perhaps women least of all) can fulfill the imaginary promise of an ideal constancy of things against which men continue unsuccessfully to measure and so define their own necessarily limited lives, thus ensuring their disappointment with its promise.

Though Simon boasts of being normally impulsive, he acknowledges the fundamentally passive nature of his personality and views his experience with the models as a "quiet parenthesis" in a life otherwise marked by the same stresses and contentiousness that affects most people. The judgment recalls his description of the affair with the poet as a detour. "I regard myself as asleep," he admits at one point, "I go along, things happen to me, there are disturbances, one copes. . ."(47).

In this understated determination, predictably, Simon looks more to the past than the present. He hopes to recapture the way of looking at all things as funny that he identifies with his youth and recalls the clownlike feeling he experienced wearing hospital scrubs at the joyful birth of his daughter. Such comic self-deprecation both sustains and qualifies his self-image. Despite the domestic arrangement, he thinks of himself as avuncular and identifies with the giraffe, a more or less nondescript if disproportioned animal who, he notes, has been neglected even by the automobile industry in choosing names for their models. Alternatively he sees himself as a palm tree, which he projects schematically as "a skinny curving vertical with lots of furor at the top" (108). At the same time, Simon cannot ignore those darker aspects of experience which do not so easily submit to unqualified admiration:

THE MANIFOLD AND DREADFUL GUISES OF ART

Simon wanted very much to be a hearty, optimistic American like the President, but on the other hand did not trust hearty, optimistic Americans, like the President. He had considered the possibility that the President, when not in public, was not really hearty and optimistic but rather a gloomy, obsessed man with a profound fear of the potentially disastrous processes in which he was enmeshed, no more sanguine than the Fisher King (58).

Simon's sober assessment of things is, then, as much the result of his fear of emotional isolation as of his intellectual detachment from conventional social patterns. Aware of the consequent appeal of a fortress as an architectural metaphor, even he is amazed to discover how many things he doesn't care about. "You're too wrapped up in your own stuff even to try. To know someone," his wife, Carol, accuses him bitterly. And in a gesture that says as much about Simon's indifference as her frustration with it she pours four quarts of ice water on him as he lies in bed. Like the end of his affair with the poet, the breakup of Simon's marriage is not accounted for other than in some hints given in brief telephone conversations both with his wife and his daughter, Sarah. Concerned more with her career than with the care of their daughter, Carol makes impossibly acquisitive demands for a divorce settlement, terms which Simon, in a characteristically passive response,

is nonetheless prepared to accept. It is Carol, however—in a passage from an *Esquire* short story "Paradise
Before the Egg," adapted from the novel but not included in the published version—who confirms the
compromises that a various if necessarily imperfect
world demands. "I understand a divided heart," she
tells Simon, who sensible of the unlikelihood of any
permanent relationship with the models resolves in the
meanwhile to listen to them.[11]

The passage into historical consciousness as responsible instead of the tragic knowledge of good and
evil, for the fortunate fall from Paradise is projected as
well in the menace and excitement that circumscribe the
urban experience against which the action of the novel
is projected. Part of that experience consists of newspaper stories warning of such unlikely threats as those
from rabid skunks, part consists of obliquely parallel
false warnings when cheap building construction
causes smoke alarms to sound. Simon mockingly identifies the contradictory nature of urban life in a headline
in the *New York Times* that proclaims, "Death May
Haunt Calcutta's Streets, But Teeming City Throbs With
Life" (21). He witnesses the brutal beating of a police-
woman and the indifference of a doctor to a drunk lying
sick in a doorway. He hears "the clamor of the street,
sirens, rape, outrage" through the open windows of his
apartment. Nonetheless, the pace of the city, its muse-
ums, department stores, theaters, restaurants, even its

THE MANIFOLD AND DREADFUL GUISES OF ART

produce stands—the very busyness and variety of its activity—combine to generate a carnival atmosphere whose joyful spontaneity Simon sees represented early one morning when a man wearing violet running shorts, who appears to be in his early forties, runs in circles carrying on his shoulders a woman of about the same age who waves her arms like a circus performer.

It is, in fact, this inclusive, nondiscriminatory contentment with the ordinary and so imperfect that circumscribes Simon's idea of Paradise, which he visualizes as populated by the angels with only one wing he has seen in an old engraving. His response characteristically is both comic and pragmatic: he imagines what kind of furniture it would be necessary to design for their celestial comfort. Though grotesquely limited, Simon is aware, one can still function. The variety possible within such limits and the satisfactions it permits are affirmed in a description one of the models gives of her experience caring for children. They were, she explains just "ordinary children. The children need a lot of work. They're just like anybody else. They need a lot of work. They're not finished. We glued things to paper plates. I worked with them. Daily. On a daily basis" (125).

Experienced primarily in passive terms ("We could sit around and watch old movies on television," Simon suggests as an alternative to one of the models who is thinking of leaving), the incomplete Paradise does not, then, so much offer an opportunity for irresponsible self-gratification as for limited if ultimately purposeless activity. Simon compares it to the day-to-day existence that marked his overseas tour of duty in the Army, a period he describes as one of well-intentioned aimlessness.

The ethical questions underlying this condition and related matters of human conduct are examined in an extended conversation between Simon and a doctor, identified only as Q and A, a reductive device Barthelme repeatedly employs to designate the speakers in his dialogue stories. Though the doctor explicitly disclaims any psychiatric credentials—psychiatry is not medicine, he says disparagingly—the exchange, which begins with an attempt to compile a medical history, soon broadens into what unmistakably resembles an encounter between patient and therapist in which the roles continue to alternate.

Initially appearing as a story in *The New Yorker* called "Basil from Her Garden," the dialogue is redistributed throughout the novel as independent chapters. There are several significant differences between the two versions. Simon's wife is given the more common name Carol rather than the somewhat exotic, Grete, she is called in the story. "Everybody's wife is named Carol," one of the models notes. That, of course, is the point. Simon's marital discord, it is thus suggested, is representative, a way marriage has come to be understood rather than, as in the story, a way the reader comes to know Simon. His affair in the story with a

THE MANIFOLD AND DREADFUL GUISES OF ART

woman named Althea is replaced presumptively by his brief interlude with the unnamed poet, and his relationship with the models further generalizes his situation. Though each model is different, none is distinctive, and in fact Simon's equal feeling for all three women suggests that they are, for the most part, interchangeable.

More striking changes occur in the development of the two men and in the style of their exchange. Q describes himself as "just sort of a regular person, one who worries about cancer a lot" (77). Along with mortality he is, in fact, concerned with the care of his aging parents and with what he terms last things. His longing for a more exciting experience is suggested in his febrile curiosity about the circumstances of A's life, which he thinks of as unique despite A's insistence that they are described by only ordinary interests.

Like Q's tasteless appreciation of out-of-the-way rock groups, such as "Echo and the Bunnymen," videos of the Tet Offensive narrated by Walter Cronkite, or his casual offer of medication to deal with the anxieties of daily life; A's sense of the ordinary proves decidedly uncommon and turns out to include bow-hunting and membership in an environmental group. Q's impatience with this information—he abruptly interrupts A's explanation of the group's activities—gives way to his demand for the recitation of even more unusual pursuits, but A continues to regard what he does as commonplace even when he casually lists adultery among his interests. Replying to Q's moralistic astonishment,

A attempts to defend the value of this very human impulse against broader, more impersonal, and ultimately indefinable principles by which society hopes to be guided, feels itself judged, and consequently experiences inadequacy and guilt: "You think about this staggering concept, the mind of God and then you think He's sitting around worrying about this guy and this woman at the Beechnut Travelodge? I think not" (77). The particularization of the common, even somewhat sleazy, name—the Beechnut Travelodge—manages to invest the adultery with a comic and yet oddly tenacious dignity, perhaps because of the awful and overwhelming blankness against which it is measured. For A, the pleasures of adultery, like those of his other activities, are determined by the same sense of neighborliness or ordinary human exchanges that he celebrates in the gift of herbs from a neighbor's garden. It is that activity which, if does not allay his fears at the ever-present threat of sudden and surprising violence, at least helps to make it possible to live with them.

The ordinary environment, it turns out, further is more various than one would suppose and indeed is discovered to be the ground for all sorts of extravagant or at least imaginative possibilities. A's impulse to join the CIA is triggered by the appearance of a recruiting ad in, of all places, the daily newspaper. Adultery, while clearly an experience of a different order, is no less a part of daily life for A than the assortment of credit cards and children's photographs in his wallet

THE MANIFOLD AND DREADFUL GUISES OF ART

and is as satisfying when indulged in as a mental exercise, as when actively consummated.

It is this ordinary quality that Q both envies and hopes to transcend. His own modest ambition to own an electric leaf blower, his ability to regulate his habits, above all perhaps, his reluctance to express emotion ("I never scream," he assures A, "I'm a doctor.") testify to the importance he places upon self-discipline. Even his fantasies take the form of exercising control. In one of them, he imagines being called to an affluent home as the representative of a pest control service. Despite the sexually suggestive situation in which he finds himself, his behavior remains impeccably professional, if symbolically onanistic and leaves a bad if temporary odor. For it, he is nonetheless rewarded with a medal and a chaste kiss on both cheeks that signals the acknowledgment of valor in combat and that, his two-word summary "Pest Control" seems to indicate, he views with more than a little irony.

Like Q, who is thus troubled by the thought that he may be satisfied with too little, A admits feeling depressed ("only a bit depressed, only a bit"). The sentiment was originally attributed to Q in *The New Yorker* story and suggests not so much a reversal as a commonality of attitudes. Mirroring the dream in which he imagined his father playing the wrong notes at a piano concert, A is concerned about his own inadequacy. "I feel that everything is being nibbled away, because I can't *get it right*—" he admits (98).

UNDERSTANDING DONALD BARTHELME

The changes from the story to the novel suggest that the dialogue comes to represent the conflicting voices of the same figure. Though A's preference in the story for frozen dinners is deleted from the novel, he is made to alternate concerns that in the story were cast as a repeated sequence of statements all attributed to Q, each revealing some aspect of his self-questioning uncertainty. Initially, for example, it is Q who points somewhat wistfully to the leaf blower as an expression of self-doubt about his ability to extend the range of his desires beyond those circumscribed by domestic and, at least in sexual circumstances, painfully naïve limits. In the novel, this observation is made by A, who thus turns it into ironic self-criticism.

Q, on the other hand, is troubled in the novel by dreams of being unable to satisfy the requirements for cleanliness of his army rifle, a further sexually suggestive anxiety. It is complemented by his abrupt concern about his ability to function as a farmer, an occupation identified with his return to the fundamental processes of nature rather than more sophisticated difficulties presented by urban life. A's contrasting view of contentment with those processes, particularly as they are represented by hotel-style living, is made suspect by the unreasonable fears he associates with such a lifestyle, particularly with the temptations for sexual adventure it offers. On the other hand, the restlessness A feels at the prospect of unlimited possibilities is objectified for him by the limitless expanse of the ocean, underscored, on one occasion, by a talkative fellow passenger who overwhelmed him with what seemed like an endless succession of anecdotes and by his own vaguely troubling experiences. Finding that he can make an appointment for a haircut at any time during what should normally be a busy Saturday morning, he asks Q with concern, "Do you think the world knows something I don't know?" (46).

The knowledge at which the conversation arrives, finally, proves to be an affirmation of the ordinary as a source of rather than an alternative to possibility. The point is made in the novel far more unambiguously than in the story, where the concluding exchange takes the following form:

Q—Transcendence is possible.
A—Yes.
Q—Is it possible?
A—Not out of the question.
Q—Is it really possible?
A—Yes. Believe me.[12]

Aside from the reversal which sets A's increasingly confident reassurances against Q's inversely fragile vulnerability, what is central to this exchange is the framing of possibility in terms of escape. In the novel, there is no mention of trancendence. Nor is there any attempt to regain Paradise. Though the models have left, A, despite troubled dreams, experiences no real sense of deprivation. On the whole he finds he is able to sleep better at least, he drily acknowledges, four or five hours a night. Q, in what appears to be an illogical jump, but one which clearly makes Barthelme's point, abruptly turns the conversation to the disturbing power of art. Though A agrees, he significantly declines Q's offer of barbiturates. And in an ambiguous ending which echoes A's experience in trying to make an appointment to get his hair cut and also the assurances, early in Barthelme's canon, given by Daumier's surrogate, that openings are always there if we can find them, both voices agree that, unaccountably, perhaps even miraculously, it feels like Saturday.

The celebratory note, it would seem, comes from the conjunction of the imaginative and the pedestrian that the models bravely sound as they leave, despite their overall bleak prospects. Veronica significantly indicates the pull of reality in her self-mocking announcement that "I gots to make mah mark in de whirl." A contrasting impulse for Ann comes not from "de whirl" but from dreams, which tell her that it's time to "Split! Split!" And finally the third model, Dore, sounds the jazzy note against which both impulses must contest. "Time boogies on," she says (206). With a motion that somewhat resembles that of Barthelme's prose, the three of them "lurch" through the door. For Simon, that hesitant movement, the small, everyday kinds of actions, like the gift of basil from his neighbor's garden, are what, at fifty-three, allow him to "enjoy the turning of the wheel." In the face of gradual aging, he is aware, renewal requires settling for movement without the expectation of progress, a commitment to competence or at least to the resilience he finds in a pregnant German woman abandoned by her American soldier-husband. Above all, such renewal takes the form of repetitive activity which fixes briefly an otherwise perishable moment, such as that, interrupted even as it is described, in which a woman is glimpsed angrily sitting on a solitary park bench, "shoulders raised, legs kicking—" (78). For Simon, it is such concrete beauty that accounts for his qualified optimism. "I have hope," he confides at one point to the models, "not a hell of a lot of hope, but some hope. You need tons of hope simply in order to function. Got to think everything will work out" (202).

That Paradise exists here or nowhere, or rather that the world with all of its dissatisfactions nonetheless provides all the matter that can be known of experience is the autumnal wisdom expressed in Barthelme's posthumously published novel, *The King*.[13] Barthelme employs many of his standard techniques of displacement so that his landscape seems at once recognizable and yet unfamiliar. Written all in dialogue, the novel updates the Arthurian legend, not only as Barthelme has done before through the use of contemporary slang or by anachronistic references, but by projecting the mythic characters and customs as part of contemporary events. Arthur not only battles against Mordred; he fights the Nazis during the Second World War, listens to commentary of Ezra Pound or Lord Haw Haw, whose broadcasts deal chiefly with court gossip concerning Guinevere and Launcelot, and quotes from Winston Churchill's inspirational rhetoric. He is interrupted in battle by a summons to jury duty, unhorsed by a mortar round, and, anticipating what may be a response from literal-minded critics, wonders whether the term "refrigerators" Sir Kay uses in a figure of speech may be too modern.

As in *Snow White*, there is in *The King* only the most oblique sense of narrative development. The novel is structured in short chapters, none more than three or four pages, that serve as the occasion for a series of meditations on a variety of subjects including aging, taxes, nuclear war (bombing is meant to be a learning experience one knight explains), adultery, the beauty of women, the history of stirrups. Infidelity is treated with casual indifference by the court, and the central issue in Mordred's rebellion is put in terms of the conflict between father and son, as much the consequence of Arthur's attempt to forestall the prophesy of his own death as of Mordred's villainous nature. "It's a fantasy," Mordred acknowledges ingenuously of his wish to overthrow his father, "I've entertained myself with it since I was a boy." The setting affords Barthelme the opportunity to indulge his interest in surprising combinations of words and phrases, and it is this movement of words that proves the real substance of the novel. Words, for Barthelme, do not so much indicate the relation to things as allow for discovery of the world through their playful interactions with one another. Accordingly, in Bartheleme's fiction, it is not the human voice that is heard but its sound, the rhythms which evoke the expression of feeling, subverting not only the arbitrary sequence of history but the discursive logic of language as well.

The King begins with a clue to the direction of Barthelme's own progress. Riding full tilt, Sir Launcelot appears at first to be headed back in the direction from which he came. Actually, as a nameless bystander notes, his direction is slightly different. "It's at an angle of about fifteen degrees to the first!" Though as he rides into the remote distance, the image of the knight grows smaller, the shift and subsequent changes in direction fail to diminish his intensity or deflect him from his unstated and still far-distant goal. Sir Launcelot's ride, like such devices as lists of absent objects (knights who leave Arthur's realm to join the rebellion), indicates an ironic distancing of the subject (irony itself requires an absence or disparity between what is said and what is meant, what is anticipated and what is realized) and at the same time establishes a presence that returns the subject to the world.

Though still disconnected from the conversations which follow them, the exchanges between the characters seem more responsive than in Barthelme's earlier dialogues, which consist of juxtaposed fragments. In a shift from both the judgmental posture and ironic tone of the early fiction, the dialogue in *The King* seems more ruminative, less precarious. In Barthelme's dialogue stories, the conditions which brought characters together, the situations in which they found themselves, even the identities of the speakers were typically left unstated so that they remained suspended in time and space and their conversations unlinked from one to the next. The authority of a narrative, as Jean-Francois Lyotard suggests, comes as much from its provenance—who tells the story and how the narrator arrives at that knowledge—as from its meaning.[14] In modern fiction, such localizing coordinates often *are* the meaning of the narrative. By leaving them blank, Barthelme displaces meaning from the abstract idea of continuity to the occurrence itself, from history to act, above all, perhaps, from the narrator to the subject of his account. In *The King,* fewer thoughts are broken off in mid-sentence. Speakers are provided with attribution, incongruities are referred back to a norm. Relations, accordingly, do begin to emerge. The novel, then, reflects an increasing mellowness in Barthelme's treatment of his themes. "I like music that is more affirmative, if I may put it that way," King Arthur declares at one point. Life, he is aware, contains dolor enough.

In one episode, a Blue Knight, whose color reflects his temperament and who has written a book called *On the Impossibility of Paradise*, attributes his melancholy to prenatal influences. In an ironic comment on such fashionable disaffection, the knight reveals that he was un-

THE MANIFOLD AND DREADFUL GUISES OF ART

happy even in the womb, where he was exposed to the discordancies of modern music and literature when his mother listened to Alban Berg's *Lulu* or read Wyndham Lewis's magazine *Blast*. What troubles the Blue Knight most, however, is the urgency conventional art imposes on experience. "Paradise, the Fall, and the return to Paradise—it's not a story," he complains. "It's too symmetrical. There are no twists. Just Paradise, zip, Fall, zip, and Paradise again, zip."

The undercutting of authority, in fiction as in life, is further challenged in Arthur's defense of the throne as a viable institution to a reporter from *The Spectator* who has come to interview him. The interview echoes the reduction of experience to textual understanding that Jane in *Snow White* attempted to bridge. Acknowledging that he speaks in the authoritative and so impersonal language of proclamation, Arthur nonetheless notes that in the same "universe of discourse" there is an equality of signs that determine leadership. As examples, he points to the king's scepter, the conductor's baton, the physician's caduceus, the magician's wand, even the writer's pencil. The difference between the person in control and the general public, he insists, is knowing how to use the symbols of leadership which, among other things, consists of acknowledging distinctions of hierarchy without allowing them to interfere with the business of running a kingdom. At the same time Arthur indicates the waste of time that goes into determining the arbitrary order of rank, and notes both the demands made on the public and its insistence on being entertained. In what is perhaps the most transparent identification with the artist, Arthur concludes with the king's need both to express and yet conceal his private life (or autobiography) of which, he insists, he cannot speak, "For if I spoke about it, it would be outer, not inner, and keeping the inner *in* is the very essence of kingship."

Barthelme clouds the relation of the author and reader with a degree of ambivalence when Sir Launcelot, in company with a Black Knight called Sir Roger de Ibadan, encounters a poacher who identifies himself as Walter the Penniless. "We don't want the extraordinary, as represented by you gentlemen and your famous king, any longer," Walter explains to the knights. "It is a time for the unexceptional, the untalented, the ordinary, the downright maladroit. Quite a large constituency. All genuine certified human beings, with hearts and souls and all the rest of it. You fellows, worshipful as you may be, are anachronisms." While the knights occupy themselves with the enjoyment of gourmet cuisine, Walter compares them to the defeat of the Polish cavalry by German tanks. "A tank," he explains, "is nothing else but an expression of the will of the hundred workers who put it together. And they shall prevail!" The identification of the common people with the German army undercuts to some degree the democractic principles with which they are otherwise identified, and Walter's subsequent prediction that the

THE MANIFOLD AND DREADFUL GUISES OF ART

knight's function will ultmately be limited to the ornamental (he foresees they will become ushers, parking
lot supervisers, doormen, elevator operators) has a certain snobbishness of its own. Still, the declaration seems
less an apology for incompetence than a recognition of
the value of the commonplace, and even the two
knights acknowledge that many of the dragons said to
have been slain proved to be merely lizards.

At one point the Black Knight's lover, Clarice, a
career woman whose calling is that of highwayman,
responds to his proposal that she go away with him.
"One thing I like about men," Clarice remarks with fond
contempt, "is that they have ideas, grand impossible
ideas, ideas like *going away*—" Her response is in part
an expression of feminist independence. Such "wonderful, sweeping, soul-replenishing ideas," Clarice adds,
"sound good for about five minutes. Until you think
about them." Pressed to give up her life of crime and
accept Sir Roger's protection, she protests that it would
be the equivalent of handing him a leash.

It is not the war between the sexes that lies at the
center of the novel, however, but what Launcelot, quoting Tennyson, identifies as "the war of Time against the
soul of man," and in this battle both knights and ladies,
both Guinevere's promiscuity and Arthur's more idealistic if naïve struggle to impose order on things, must
submit the claims of imagination to those of reality.
Arthur does astonish the populace watching him fish
on a barren plain by actually catching something. For

imagination, there is always the possibility of a miracle. But the myth-creating queen, as Guinevere is called, at length finds her powers of enchantment insufficient to keep her lovers. Despite a leaky roof, the royal couple finds at least some measure of contentment in the picture of domesticity with which the novel ends, and even Launcelot grows tired and finds that the structure of romance may be only a dream he dreamed under an apple tree. The dream is one of elegance. It begins as Guinevere approaches elaborately gowned and carrying an expensive bottle of wine—Barthelme does not neglect to specify the wine as Pinot Grigio—and ends, and perhaps begins again, with the apple tree.

Notes

1. Christopher Finch, *The Art of Walt Disney: From Mickey Mouse to the Magic Kingdoms* (New York: Abrams, 1983) 169.

2. John Leland, "Remarks Re-marked: Barthelme, What Curios of Signs!" *Boundary* 2 5 (Spring 1977): 795–811. In probing the limits of language, Leland argues that Barthelme mocks traditional literary expectations and in so doing forces us to reexamine our conventions of making sense and in particular our way of reading signs including those of "literature."

3. *Snow White* (New York: Atheneum, 1972). Further references will be noted parenthetically in the text.

4. Sally McNall, "'But Why Am I Troubling Myself About Cans?': Style, Reaction, and Lack of Reaction in Barthelme's *Snow White*," *Language and Style* 8 (1974): 81–94.

THE MANIFOLD AND DREADFUL GUISES OF ART

5. Philip Stevick, "Prolegomena to the Study of Fictional Dreck," *Alternate Pleasures: Postrealist Fiction and the Tradition* (Urbana: University of Illinois Press, 1981) 122–42.

6. Henry James, "The Art of Fiction," in *"The Art of Fiction" and Other Essays,* intro. Morris Roberts (New York: Oxford UP, 1948) 13.

7. John Carlos Rowe, *The Theoretical Dimensions of Henry James* (Madison: The University of Wisconsin Press, 1984) 11.

8. James 11. In a markedly different interpretation, Gerald Graff points to this passage in support of his argument that in inverting James's concern for the principle of artistic selection, Barthelme "operates by a law of equivalance according to which nothing is intrinsically more interesting than anything else." In Barthelme's consequent focus on language as the novel's chief subject, Graff concludes, canned goods become the equivalent in his work of moral choice. See Gerald Graff, *Literature Against Itself: Literary Ideas in Modern Society* (Chicago: University of Chicago Press, 1979), 53.

9. *The Dead Father* (New York: Farrar, 1975) 42–43. Further references will be noted parenthetically in the text.

10. *Paradise* (New York: Putnam's, 1986) 30. Further references will appear parenthetically in the text.

11. "Paradise Before the Egg," *Esquire* (August 1986): 51.

12. "Basil from Her Garden," *The New Yorker* 61 (21 October, 1985): 39.

13. I am grateful to Kathy Walton Banks and Edward Burlingame Books of Harper & Row for graciously allowing me to examine galley proofs of the novel.

14. Jean-Francois Lyotard, *The Postmodern Condition: A Report on Knowledge,* (Minneapolis: University of Minnesota Press, 1984) 18–23.

CHAPTER FIVE

These Balloons Have a Right to Be Heard

Even in the novel, which conventionally demands extended narrative development, Barthelme has adopted the anecdotal structure of unrelated incident. There is little attempt to enact or to represent the world in its thickness or, alternatively, to reduce that world to a metafictional gesture which locates reality only in the act of expressing it. Nothing in his stories suggests that the characters even suspect a world outside their own in which a different set of conditions obtain. Even his clichéd conversations have the objective or ritualized quality of, say, Hemingway's metaphors of sports or Faulkner's stylized genealogies of agrarian society that attempt to set recognizable limits to human exchanges and so impart to them an ethical dimension.

Though Barthelme's use of such cultural references reflects an interest in the surface of experience rather than its symbolic resonance, his writing falls within that tendency Philip Stevick identifies as formally serious but unmistakably funny in which there is a shift "from the ironic and distanced voice of the modernists to the

THESE BALLOONS HAVE A RIGHT TO BE HEARD

naive, involved, vulnerable voice of the postmodernists"[1] Nonetheless, Barthelme has been able to invest his fictions with a cultural immediacy paradoxically without distinguishing between historical periods or even between the characters in his fiction and the objects they move among. The schools at which people are educated, the cars they drive, the neighborhoods in which they live, the restaurants where they eat, the clothes they wear say little about what these figures are like or what value to put on the way they behave. The reader can't be certain what to make of the sadness or joy that results from what a character does or doesn't do while all actions only vaguely resemble, but never accurately depict, those that take place in actual, or even the fictive, distortions through which the world is conventionally viewed and understood. Drawing upon the world but not imitating it, Barthelme's fictive inventions are abstract yet figural and generate a turbulence which results from the attempt to capture the movement of things, or the changes they undergo, under the pressure of words even more than of time.

As a result, what happens in one part of the story does not necessarily account for events which occur in another but more often replicates them very much in the manner of the question-and-answer exchanges that glance off each other in what seem at first ironic confrontations, but which prove at length equally vulnerable expressions of the inability to advance the narrative. Fiction and nonfiction accordingly are merged into a distinctly contemporary form marked by the overall breakdown of generic distinctions—distinctions between popular and literary cultural forms, between longer and short fictions, between fiction and other esthetic disciplines, in sum a tendency toward homogenization. Though embedded with recognizable names and places and with jargon identifying various social and vocational fields, Barthelme's fiction does not arrive at closure by answering the proposed questions of whether the central figure will successfully complete the task he sets for himself at the beginning or discover something more important along the way or even what the significance was of the whole enterprise. The elimination of a point of view through which the action can be interpreted, the shift or lack of identification of speakers, the neutral backgrounds against which events are said to occur and into which they blend, the lists (which seemingly invert the democratic inclusiveness found in American writers from Melville and Whitman to Saul Bellow) all contribute to a leveling not only of experience but of narrative itself.

Unlike the single actions that historically governed short fiction, Barthelme's stories accommodate any number of centers of interest, all equally emphasized. Even the flow of Barthelme's sentences is uneven, often interrupted or left incomplete, choked by irrelevant detail or given an opaque linguistic texture by sudden shifts in meaning or in the direction of thought. The displacement of the transparency through which language formerly established a correspondence between private values and communal experience results in, among other things, the undercutting of the ability to visualize what is happening. It is surprising, then, that Barthelme's stories do not respond to the standard fictive intention to make the reader see. What they attempt is to make necessary a reexamination of the images that have come to take the place of vision.

Perhaps most surprising of all is that this tendency emerges as well in those stories which contain the illustrations, engravings, unusual typographical arrangements, or even drawings Barthelme sometimes playfully appends to his text. Barthelme has accounted for this tendency, which he acknowledges as a yearning for something painters can do that is "not properly the domain of writers," by suggesting that it affords "an immediate impact—a beautifully realized whole that can be taken in at a glance and yet still be studied for a long time."[2] More persuasively, the graphics call attention to the physicality of the written medium, which, Barthelme has explained, constitute what he had the narrator in "See the Moon" view enviously as a "fantastic metaphysical advantage."[3]

Though they may be found in such stories as "The Flight of Pigeons from the Palace" or "At the Tolstoy Museum," this graphic play is for the most part concentrated in the collection *Guilty Pleasures* (1979) and dramatically drops off thereafter. Having read a review of *Great Days* in which the reviewer commented with relief that the book had no pictures, Barthelme decided that he had exhausted the impact afforded by the combination of words and pictures.[4] In the preface to *Guilty Pleasures*, Barthelme has labeled what it contains as parodies, satires (frequently political), "brokeback fables," and even "bastard reportage," and has designated the entire collection as nonfiction. That they were occasional pieces, that is, written in response to a specific circumstance (or perhaps irritation), suggests not only a close relationship to reality but a sense of incompleteness without such reference which the nonsense of the story itself works to frustrate. At the same time, it makes clear that these pieces will be subject to the same expectations or lack of them as narrative fiction and informed by the same strategy of collapsing disparate objects into a single plane of reality.

"Down the Line with the Annual," a parody of a consumer bulletin's claim to widespread acceptance by being included as part of a high school or even college curriculum, makes passing reference to a reading list that includes Herodotus, Saint-Simon, and Rilke, and ends with Owen Wister. It illustrates the dangers of slow-drying ink with the narrator's experience of having his letters "bleed through their envelopes like the hands of a medieval saint" (*Guilty Pleasures* 5). As these extravagant rhetorical devices suggest, the object of the piece is not merely an attack on consumerism or even the literary pretentiousness of the journal. It is more than anything an opportunity to confirm in the succes-

THESE BALLOONS HAVE A RIGHT TO BE HEARD

sion of products named the substantiality of the world in which they exist so that the humor turns against itself in the narrator Charles's concluding resolve to escape it along with his killer hawk and a woman named Candace, who has been victimized both by the annual and by the defective products it warns against. What needs to be emphasized, however, is the equally ludicrous extravagance of the alternative Charles proposes to claustrophobic consumerism. "And now Port Moresby," he concludes in a stylistic echo of S. J. Perelman, "Come Candace, let me coax you out from under that bell jar, into which you have repaired to guard delicate ears against sound of china crazing in the kitchen" (8).

The object of these satires, then, is style, often as it translates itself into journalistic pretension. In "L'Lapse," subtitled "A Scenario for Michelangelo Antonioni," the parody is not merely of the sixties new-wave Italian cinema but of the film criticism it generated. "That Cosmopolitan Girl" and "Snap Snap," two other pieces in the collection, are satires respectively of the italic breathlessness of women's fashion magazines and the equally exaggerated urgency of news magazines. "Games Are the Enemies of Beauty, Truth, and Sleep, Amanda Said," concerns itself as a story not only with the trivialization of the history, preoccupations, and social pretentions of the culture and the resulting boredom and aimlessness (a subject ironically alluded to in "Kierkegaard Unfair to Schlegel") but with the way it comically attempts to impose structure and so meaning on that activity by inventing models or lifelike representations of it (though a concluding game, "Ennui," built on the absence of games, slyly reestablishes the value of such distractions at the expense of the eponymous heroine's rejection of them).

In "The Expedition," a series of illustrations purportedly relate the history of an expedition to the polar region which results in the discovery of an object designated the largest of its kind, but which, despite an illustration that might be anything from a lampshade to a clamshell, is not otherwise identified. Like the photographic negative of Tolstoy in "At the Tolstoy Museum," or the two photographs labeled Fig. 1 and Fig. 2 in "The Photographs," which are described as photographs of the human soul taken by the first spacecraft to navigate the outer solar system but actually resemble shards unearthed during an archeological dig, the illustrations in "The Expedition" do not serve as a model of mimetic representation (this is not the way Tolstoy might have looked, e.g.). Rather they constitute a reality of their own (this is the way a picture of Tolstoy looks).

Barthelme comes at the question of illustration directly in "The Photographs," which develops as one of Barthelme's dialogue stories where both speakers more or less condone the affair one is having with the other's wife (and as a corollary the need to burn the photographs of the soul) as a means of sustaining a necessary uncertainty in life, if only momentarily. Barthelme's point, is not an attack on certainty, but quite the opposite, a comment on the extraordinary lengths to which people will go, or feel they are entitled to go, in avoiding the ordinary way of regarding experience.

In "The Expedition," this focus on perception reverses the conventional relation between text and illustration. It is the caption itself that becomes the subject of, really the occasion for, the illustration not the supposed event depicted. Such interaction does not work to the exclusion of reality. It denies the possibility of reducing it to a fixed image or attitude. Illustration thus serves as a reality of its own equal to that of the text for which it stands almost as a metaphor. What Barthelme's inversion does is dissociate the metaphor from an exclusively linguistic world, where it serves to translate human or instinctive or mechanical attributes from one kind of symbol to another, and locate it instead in a depicted world of formal representations.

When the word or the text no longer alludes to or represents an external reality beyond itself, when, that is, it constitutes an invention created from recognizable elements but clearly not meant to be mistaken for the way those elements are combined in the world; the possibility of a norm is itself withdrawn and the depicted world becomes an expression of sheer fun. In "A Nation on Wheels" the satire is a commentary upon a tire manufacturer's advertisng boast that America has become a nation of wheels, and it treats this mild hyperbole literally by juxtaposing photographic images of outsized rubber tires against human figures or statuary of greatly reduced scale. In one case the wheels are made to support an ice-cream cone done in the style of a Roy Lichtenstein painting. In another a woman dressed in the costume of the 1890s tearfully reacts to the news of this technological revolution. In a third, a fencer roughly one-third their size lunges at two enormous whitewall tires. In a concluding illustration a semicircle of boys dressed in jockey silks and caps, and displaying hoops, surround a man in a bowler who holds his hand to his mouth as though calling instructions to them. Behind the jockeys stands a group of young spectators, and far in the background is the outline of what appears to be large houses or hotels. The caption for the illustration is "A class in wheel appreciation." The elaborate setting of these illustrations for so small and repetitious a joke should not obscure what is perhaps a more central concern, one that addresses itself to narrative at least as much as cultural posture. Along with a sense of the guilty pleasure Barthelme enjoys at mounting pictures in incongruous contexts, these pieces lead us, perhaps inadvertently, to the distortion that occurs when representation concentrates on linguistic distinctions to the exclusion of the literal world.

A clue to the value of the literal in opposing illusionism is provided in a series of pieces Barthelme wrote for the "Notes and Comments" section of *The New Yorker* and collected under the title *Here in the Village*.

THESE BALLOONS HAVE A RIGHT TO BE HEARD

The subjects typically are carefully observed but disconnected events that occur during the narrator's travels around Greenwich Village where Barthelme lived, or more playful fantasies which his exposure to its idiosyncracies and those of society at large give rise. As part of the ordinary occasion, he encounters the unlikely facts: a steel-gray bulldog with a flower in its collar, a multiracial high school band of surprising competence, a laundromat bulletin board that serves as the "jungle drums of the Village," a man insulated in Reynolds Wrap to make sleeping in his automobile more comfortable, a meeting with Norman Mailer dressed in a powder blue safari suit, the magic-marker decorations of a pizza-parlor window, the going-out-of-business sale of a landmark bakery, an imagined consultation with a fortune teller who wears Hermes scarves and uses IBM punchcards to foretell the future. None of these, however, confuses the absence of meaning with the absence of a reality outside that of the text or confines that reality to the activity or process of writing through which it is structured. Rather they attempt to exploit the informational ellipses to confirm the existence of an experiential world, particularly in its more ephemeral or popular forms. It is, in fact, the loss of that world or the presumption of its loss, often as a result of equating it with absence or decontextualization, that accounts for the satiric tone of much of Barthelme's writing and serves as its object. Detachment from the pragmatic, for example, results in an almost paralyzing isolation for the theologian Thomas Brecker in "January," (*Forty Stories*), a parody of the interview that stays so close to the form it imitates that much of the point of the story lies in frustrating the conventional expectations of parody. The reader waits in vain for some indication of the interviewer's fatuousness or of Brecker's pompous sense of self-importance. Instead, somewhat like St. Anthony in Barthelme's "The Temptation of St. Anthony," the skeptical theologian seems perceptive, knowledgeable, thoughtful, modest to the point of self-effacement. "I have a lifelong tendency," he admits, "not to want to be absorbed into the universal."[5] Brecker's notion of the value of rejecting society's demand for the extraordinary, his turning from what he describes as the "madness of crowds," leads, as he is aware, to a refusal of certain relations with others and so to an isolation and self-questioning that makes it increasingly difficult to exist in the world. Though Brecker affirms the uniqueness of individual being, the fear of submitting the expectations of the self to the limits imposed by culture, as he is further aware, carries with it an unwillingness to submit to any limits, even those of understanding. While, as he knows, in Eastern religions such rejection of finitude allows a marvelous serenity, it dissolves the tense caution that, in part, also defines humanity.

Brecker's humane self-searching carries its own penalties. The story takes its title from his speculating on the consequences of altering the conventional—the mnemonic for the number of days in each month—so that rather than 31 days January is arbitrarily given none. This change, he argues, would itself generate a convention that in turn would perpetuate its own error. Though seemingly an argument that challenges the authority of convention, Brecker had begun his career as a journalist doing routine assignments and so developed a respect for the practical way of looking at things. Any normative tradition, he argues, can be understood only within the terms of its own historical particularity. Brecker is aware that there is no such things as a disinterested objectivity. His aversion to norms is not so much to their actuality as to the forms in which that actuality is structured. Accordingly, in a declaration that applies broadly to writing as well as to the theological matter to which Brecker refers, he insists, "There's no progress in my field, there's adding-on but nothing that can truthfully be described as progress" (255).

This attempt to accommodate the variables that make up his sense of reality to the acknowledgment of particularity does not reject the actuality of things but rather the rigidities of form to which they have been confined. Even here Brecker does not pretend to have resolved matters, admitting that one of the pleasures his profession is that it leaves him always in doubt. Though, at length, he drifts into a series of self-troubling answers for which questions are no longer even being asked, his anxiety about death and the consequent need for faith or for confirmation of meaning from some external sources is mediated finally only by locating them in relation to some concrete achievement outside the abstractions to which, he is afraid, his life's work may have been addressed.

In "Tickets," one of Barthelme's most recent stories, the narrator begins by announcing "I have decided to form a new group and am now contemplating the membership, the prospective membership, of my new group."[6] The story ends with the further explanation, "My group will be unlike any existing group, will exist in contradistinction to all existing groups, over against all existing groups, will be in fine an anti-group, given the ethos of our city, the hysterical culture of our city" (34). Immediately striking is the repetition which, along with the exaggerated attempts at precise nominal discrimination, even to the absence of pronouns, suggests the speaker wants to make sure he will not be separated from the solid world by the general atmosphere of hysteria that seems to inform it. At the same time, the strategy evokes the cold maneuvering for civility that often accompanies domestic quarrels of the most vicious nature and, in fact, just such tension does surface between the narrator and his wife, whose fondness for the symphony he regards as largely pretentious.

The ethos of the city and of the social and art worlds in which the narrator travels is further suggested by Barbet, a painter who superimposes the work of one famous artist upon that of another so as to cancel both. Even the local museum, which houses many of his paintings, adopts the postmodern architecture of quota-

THESE BALLOONS HAVE A RIGHT TO BE HEARD

tion which the narrator describes at once as provincial and "quite grand, with its old part done in the classical mode and its new part done in a mode that respects the classical mode to the point of being indistinguishable from the classical mode but is also fresh, new, contemporary, and ironic" (33).

Barbet, the narrator's wife, her friend Morton, even the narrator, all maneuver to establish themselves as arbiters of social judgment. The narrator, in particular, is concerned largely with gossip and with maintaining social distinctions. Nonetheless his group, he explains, will be formed for the purpose of demonstrating the kind of pointless enthusiasm he identifies with the workers at car washes "who are forever shouting 'Let's go!' 'Let's go!' to inspirit their fellows" (34). The shouting and the excitement they generate is, of course, to some degree a self-justifying echo of that in the wider urban society the narrator anatomizes. And the eclectic, even somewhat romantic composition of the group he intends to form—it includes a Gypsy girl and a blind man in addition to himself and his wife—mirrors to some extent that society and the jargon, artistic rivalries, and concerns about fashion that define its interest in art. But if indiscriminate, the enthusiasm is no less real, and while the groups or social cliques can only imitate its energy, there is something finally vital about its expression.

Typical of *The New Yorker*, the tone is partly bemused acceptance, partly elegant self-mockery, achieved largely through a mixture of baroque literary expression, self consciously folksy cliché, and deadpan quotation of what passes for conversational exchange in which is embedded jargon from the worlds of advertising, art, music, entertainment, or such relatively esoteric sciences as computer or audio technology. A terse understatement serving almost as a caption reduces an elaborate succession of remarks to a single, concrete image, but even this tells us little other than that some object exists, some event has occurred. In short, while ostensibly standing for taste and discrimination, the style qualifies without defining both by a catholicity of reference whose unassimilated objects ultimately receive a collective benediction and whose distortions are in no way distinguished from any proposed norms but rather are incorporated into them.

Several of the tendencies described above seem to converge in a short untitled piece that takes the form of a letter to an unnamed literary critic. Barthelme reviews the transience of literary movements dating back to plainsong in the tenth century and ending with postmodernism, which he anticipates will give way to some as yet undefined entity he tentatively designates "Revolution of the Word II" or "New Revolution of the Word." Framed as a letter to a literary critic, the piece comments in passing on the death of modernism, new criticism, existentialism, structuralism, and surrealism, in which the loss of abrasiveness toward the end resulted in "the wine of life turning into Gatorade."[7]

THESE BALLOONS HAVE A RIGHT TO BE HEARD

Barthelme here underscores his dislike for the French Nouveau Roman of Robbe-Grillet, which, he claims, "made dreariness into a religion," and though he acknowledges that "a neat omission usually raises the hairs on the back of my neck," he complains that he did not even like what was left out.[8]

Barthelme slyly attributes the decline of these movements at least as much to their acceptance by the culture as to their irrelevance. It is their fashionableness more than the superficiality of the terms that invites the satire. Noting that the anti-novel, along with the anti-hero and anti-heroine, is dead, Barthelme observes that their anti-children have been enrolled at Dalton, an East Side prep school. Bartheleme does not discuss the characteristics of these movements or identify the notable figures associated with them. A concluding catalog provides yet another of his lists of negative presence:

The Novel of the Soil is dead as are Expressionism, Impressionism, Futurism, Vorticism, Regionalism, Realism, and the Kitchen Sink School of Drama, the Theatre of the Absurd, the Theatre of Cruelty, Black Humor, and Gongorism. You know all this; I'm just totting up. To be a Pre-Raphaelite in the present era is to be somewhat out of touch. And, of course, Concrete Poetry (39).

In a similar piece on institutional or, as he terms it, non-product advertising, called "The Case of the Vanishing Product" that Barthelme did for *Harper's* in 1960, the absence of things does not necessarily mean their nonexistence. Looking at an *Annual of Advertising and Editorial Art and Design,* Barthelme notices

an intense preoccupation with objects: keys, clocks, corkscrews, kiosks, balloons, musical instruments, stones, telephones, birdcages, wineglasses, eggs, chairs, cups and saucers, pinball machines, Greek statues, old buildings, whisk brooms, candles, dice, giant strawberries. None of these things is being offered for sale. Instead they are the means by which we are to conceive of other things which *are* being offered for sale—typically nowhere in sight. The very high level of abstraction in contemporary advertising both confers a new freedom upon designers and increases the possibility of ambiguity in its use.[9]

Abstraction, then, in art as in life, may obscure connections without eliminating the very real presence of the abstract image itself. Worrying about women in yet another of the untitled Village sketches, which appeared originally as the introduction to an art exhibit, Barthelme concludes that, like such fabulous animals as the manticore, the hippogriff, or the anti-lion, woman does not exist. "What exists in the space 'woman' would occupy, if she existed," he writes, "is a concatenation of ideas about women." The ideas, however, form themselves into a presence of their own. Barthelme invites the reader to:

THESE BALLOONS HAVE A RIGHT TO BE HEARD

Imagine a net as big as a sea stretching from the Advanced Palaeolithic to the present time. Imagine human beings standing along the circumference of the net, doing their best to support it—the mighty effort, the colossal straining. Yet the animal escapes. And a strange thing happens. The net becomes the animal.[10]

"Art, touching mysteries, tends to darken rather than illuminate them," Barthelme concludes, adding that "artists enrich and complicate (whatever else they may also be doing)" (43–44). Such complications are themselves often the source of pleasure, a reassurance of solidity in the face of the often ghostly shapes into which fiction necessarily transforms things. Though Barthelme has consistently looked to writing as an escape or at least a distraction from the distortions and anxieties of reality, blending fact and fiction in a way that makes it difficult to distinguish between them, the inclusiveness itself parodies its own intent at least as much as the objects it seems to imitate. As such, its stylized exaggeration betrays a deeper intent than that simply of ironic distancing. "What do you think is the proper response to the world?" an interviewer once asked Barthelme. "Embracing it," he replied.[11] The advice is echoed in the unlikely person of a supermarket manager who serves as a marriage confidant in "Jaws," another of the previously uncollected stories which appears in *Forty Stories*. In it a woman, Natasha, shows her affection for her husband William by biting him.

Domestic felicity here, as throughout Barthelme's fiction, is hard to come by. The bites are damaging, one of them, a "real gorilla bite" severs a tendon just above the knee and leaves William with a permanent limp. Still, passion even in this runaway form proves preferable to the verbal exchanges that contain "so many terrible sentences [which] drift in the air between them, sentences about who is right and sentences about who works hardest and sentences about money and even sentences about physical appearance—the most ghastly of known sentences" (63). What Natasha's bites, like Barthelme's sentences, want to say is *Wake up! Remember!* Though the narrator maintains that what must be remembered is the ideal totality of which we are only imperfect copies, he sends William reminders of the prosaic world: a paper bag of bagels and a plastic container of cream cheese with shallots. Natasha gets a store check-cashing application preapproved. "Who can imagine anything better than everyday reality?" one can imagine Barthelme asking with only partial irony. "Who would be foolish enough to want to try?" Despite the great themes of sadness and loss that continue to surface throughout his fiction, perhaps the greatest loss, it makes clear, would be that of the world to the illusions about it which fiction is often made to represent.

THESE BALLOONS HAVE A RIGHT TO BE HEARD

Notes

1. Philip Stevick, *Alternative Pleasures: Postrealist Fiction and the Tradition* (Urbana: University of Illinois Press, 1981) 140.

2. Larry McCaffery, "Donald Barthelme," *Anything Can Happen: Interviews with Contemporary American Novelists,* ed. Tom LeClair and Larry McCaffery (Urbana: University of Illinois Press, 1983) 39.

3. McCaffery 36.

4. J.D.O'Hara, "Donald Barthelme: The Art of Fiction LXVI," *Paris Review* 80 (1981): 208.

5. "January," *Forty Stories* (New York: Putnam's, 1987) 254. Further references will be given parenthetically in the text.

6. "Tickets," *The New Yorker* 65, 6 Mar. 1989: 32.

7. *Here in the Village* (Northridge, CA: Lord John Press, 1978) 39. Much of this piece was incorporated into Barthelme's essay "Not-Knowing," in the form of a letter from one literary critic, who "sunlights" as a Parks Department employee, to another who is employed as a guard at the Whitney Museum.

8. *Here in the Village* 41.

9. "The Case of the Vanishing Product," *Harper's* (Oct. 1961): 30.

10. Jo Brans, "Donald Barthelme: Embracing the World," *Southwest Review* 67 (Spring 1982): 132.

BIBLIOGRAPHY

Works by Donald Barthelme
Novels
Snow White. New York: Atheneum, 1967. London: Cape, 1968.
The Dead Father. New York: Farrar, 1975.
Paradise. New York: Putnam's, 1986. London: Routledge, 1987.
The King. New York: Harper & Row, 1990.
Collections of Short Fiction
Come Back, Dr. Caligari. Boston: Little, Brown, 1964. London:
    Eyre & Spottiswoode, 1966.
Unspeakable Practices, Unnatural Acts. New York: Farrar, 1968,
    London: Cape, 1969.
City Life. New York: Farrar, 1970. London: Cape, 1971
Sadness. New York: Farrar, 1972. London: Cape, 1973.
Amateurs. New York: Farrar, 1976. London: Routledge, 1977.
Great Days. New York: Farrar, 1979. London: Routledge, 1979.
Sixty Stories. New York: Putnam's, 1981. London: Secker &
    Warburg, 1989.
Overnight to Many Distant Cities. New York: Putnam's, 1983.
Forty Stories. New York: Putnam's, 1987. London: Secker &
    Warburg, 1987.
Collections of Non-Fiction
Guilty Pleasures. New York: Farrar, 1974.

BIBLIOGRAPHY

Here in the Village. Northridge, CA: Lord John Press, 1978.

Children's Books

The Slightly Irregular Fire Engine, or The Hithering Thithering Djinn. New York: Farrar, 1971.

Sam's Bar: An American Landscape [with Seymour Chwast]. Garden City, NY: Doubleday, 1987.

Selected Uncollected Short Stories

"Man's Face." *The New Yorker* 40, 30 May 1964: 29.

"Then." *Mother* 3 Nov.-Dec. 1964: 22–23.

"Blue Flower Problem." *Harvest* May 1967: 29.

"Philadelphia." *The New Yorker* 44, 30 Nov. 1968: 56–58.

"Newsletter." *The New Yorker* 11 July 1970: 23.

"Adventure." *Harper's Bazaar* Dec. 1970: 92–95.

"The Story Thus Far." *The New Yorker* 47, 1 May 1971: 42–45.

"Natural History." *Harper's* 243, Aug. 1971: 44–45.

"Edwards, Amelia." *The New Yorker* 48, 9 Sept. 1972: 34–36.

"Three." *Fiction* 1 (1972): 13.

"A Man." *The New Yorker* 48, 30 Dec. 1972: 26–27.

"The Inauguration." *Harper's* 246, Jan. 1973: 86–87.

"You Are Cordially Invited." *The New Yorker* 49, 23 July 1973: 33–34.

"The Bed." *Viva*, Mar. 1974: 68–70.

"The Dassaud Prize." *The New Yorker* 51, 12 Jan. 1976: 26–29.

"Presents." *Penthouse*, Dec. 1977: 107–109.

"Momma." *The New Yorker* 54, 2 Oct. 1978: 32–33.

"Basil from Her Garden." *The New Yorker* 61, 21 Oct. 1985: 36–39.

"Tickets." *The New Yorker* 65, 6 Mar. 1989: 32–34.

Uncollected Articles and Reviews

"A Note on Elia Kazan." University of Houston *Forum* 1 (Jan. 1957): 19–22.

BIBLIOGRAPHY

"Mr. Hunt's Wooly Alpaca." [Review of *Alpaca* by H. L. Hunt] *The Reporter* 22 14 Apr. 1960: 44–46.

"The Emerging Figure." University of Houston *Forum* 3 (Summer 1961): 23–24.

"The Case of the Vanishing Product." *Harper's 223*, Oct. 1961: 30–32.

"After Joyce." *Location* 1 (Summer 1964): 14–16.

"The Tired Terror of Graham Greene." [Review of *The Comedians* by Graham Greene], *Holiday*, Apr. 1966: 146, 148–49.

"The Elegance is Under Control." [Review of *The Triumph* by John Kenneth Galbraith], *New York Times Book Review* 21 Apr. 1968, 4–5.

"The Current Cinema: Parachutes in the Trees." *The New Yorker 55*, 17 Sept. 1979: 132,134–35.

"The Current Cinema: Special Devotions." *The New Yorker 55*, 24 Sept. 1979: 132–33.

"The Current Cinema: Dead Men Comin' Through." *The New Yorker 55*, 1 Oct. 1979: 103–04.

"The Current Cinema: Three Festivals." *The New Yorker 55*, 8 Oct. 1979: 164, 167–68.

"The Current Cinema: Peculiar Influences." *The New Yorker 55*, 15 Oct. 1979: 182–83.

"Not-Knowing." *The Georgia Review* 39 (Fall 1985): 509–22.

Interviews

Baker, John F. "PW Interviews Donald Barthelme." *Publishers' Weekly*, 11 Nov. 1974: 6–7.

Brans, Jo. "Donald Barthelme: Embracing the World." *Southwest Review* 67 (Spring 1982): 121–137. Rpt. *Listen to the Voices: Conversations with Contemporary Writers*. Dallas: Southern Methodist UP, 1988. 77–101.

Klinkowitz, Jerome, "An Interview with Donald Barthelme.

BIBLIOGRAPHY

The New Fiction: Interviews with Innovative American Writers.
Ed. Joe David Bellamy. Urbana: University of Illinois Press,
1974. 45–54.

McCaffery, Larry. "An Interview with Donald Barthelme."
*Anything Can Happen: Interviews with Contemporary American
Novelists.* Ed. Thomas LeClair and Larry McCaffery. Ur-
bana: University of Illinois Press, 1982.

O'Hara, J.D. "Donald Barthelme: The Art of Fiction LXVI."
Paris Review 80 (1981): 180–210.

Schickel, Richard. "Freaked Out on Barthelme." *New York
Times Magazine* 16 Aug. 1970: 14–15, 54.

Selected Works About Barthelme
Bibliographies and Checklists

McCaffery, Larry. "Donald Barthelme, Robert Coover, William H. Gass: Three Checklists." *Bulletin of Bibliography* 31
(1974): 101–06.

Klinkowitz, Jerome, Asa Pieratt, and Robert Murray Davis.
*Donald Barthelme: A Comprehensive Bibliography and Annotated
Secondary Checklist.* Hamden, CT: Shoe String Press, 1977.

Books

Couturier, Maurice and Regis Durand. *Donald Barthelme.* London: Methuen, 1982. Argues that though the language of
Barthelme's fiction destabilizes meaning, their playful dis-
placements suspend his fiction between a minimalist concern for survival and an attempt at reconstruction.

Gordon, Lois. *Donald Barthelme.* Boston: G. K. Hall, 1981. Brief
discussions and description of Barthelme's novels and stories up to *Great Days.*

Molesworth, Charles. *Donald Barthelme's Fiction: The Ironist
Saved From Drowning.* Columbia, MO: University of Mis-

BIBLIOGRAPHY

souri Press, 1982. Neither wholly rejecting nor assenting to the contemporary world, Barthelme ironically keeps in equilibrium the longing for wholeness and meaning and the reality of fragmented culture.

Stengel, Wayne B. *The Shape of Art in the Short Stories of Donald Barthelme*. Baton Rouge: Louisiana State UP, 1985. Develops a typology that classifies Barthelme's short stories into categories dealing with identity, dialogue, society, and art. Stengel examines the strategies Barthelme employs to develop these categories such as a playful skepticism about the characters' efforts to know and understand their world; a repetitive treatment of the gestures and conversations of a narcissistic culture; and, most importantly, the attempt of surrogates to "affirm a vision of life created in their own art."

Selected Articles and Parts of Books

Achilles, Jochen. "Donald Barthelme's Aesthetic of Inversion: Caligari's Come-Back as Caligari's Leave-Taking." *The Journal of Narrative Technique* 12 (Spring 1982): 120. Achilles finds in the film *Das Cabinet des Dr. Caligari* a paradigm of the technique of inversion, or undercutting its own authority, that Barthelme himself inverts, particularly in his application of it to the writer's relation to the reader, the relation of art and reality, and the authority even of the text itself.

Ditsky, John M. "'With Ingenuity and Hard Work, Distracted': The Narrative Style of Donald Barthelme." *Style* 9 (Summer 1975): 388–400. Focuses on *Snow White*, "Daumier," and "Nothing: A Preliminary Account" to illustrate Barthelme's surrealistic fusion of details into an imitative style that uses collage to call attention to the process out of which it evolves.

BIBLIOGRAPHY

Gass, William H. "The Leading Edge of the Trash Phenomenon," *Fiction and the Figures of Life.* New York: Knopf. 1970, 97–103. Concentrates on *Unspeakable Practices, Unnatural A Acts* to show that in dealing with the themes of apathy and violence Barthelme constructs a single plane of style and value out of linguistic trash.

Gillen, Francis. "Donald Barthelme's City: A Guide." *Twentieth Century Literature* 18 (1972): 37–44. Concludes that along with the artist, dwellers in Barthelme's city struggle with the abstractions of technology (and, in particular, the media) and the world of fact in an attempt to balance a retreat toward cynical irony with the frustrations caused by the failure to distinguish between image and reality.

Hicks, Jack. "Metafiction and Donald Barthelme," *In the Singer's Temple: Prose Fictions of Barthelme, Gaines, Brautigan, Piercy, Kesey, and Kosinski.* Chapel Hill: University of North Carolina Press, 1981. 18–82. Maintains that though in works such as *Amateurs* and *Great Days* Barthelme has turned to the conditions of urban society, his fiction is essentially private, reflecting the views of French phenomenologists Georges Poulet and Gabriel Marcel which question the ability of fiction to reveal anything outside the artifice of linguistic structure.

Johnson, R.E., Jr. "Bees Barking in the Night: The End and the Beginning of Donald Barthelme's Narrative." *Boundary 2*, 5 (1977): 71–92. Drawing on "The Balloon," and "The Glass Mountain," among other stories, Johnson accounts for the difficulties of determining the beginnings and endings of Barthleme's stories as a function of the ambivalence of language that retracts any statement that might afford closure while proposing its own processes as a subject.

BIBLIOGRAPHY

Klinkowitz, Jerome. "Donald Barthelme's Art of Collage." *The Practice of Fiction in America*. Ames: Iowa State UP, 1980. 106–113. Like the Abstract Expressionist painters or contemporary poets such as Frank O'Hara, Barthelme "defamiliarizes objects by presenting them in unusual contexts."

———.*The Self-Apparent Word: Fiction as Language, Language as Fiction*. Carbondale: Southern Illinois UP, 1984. 14–15, 30–32, 71–75 and passim. Barthelme's work illustrates a "new aesthetic of reflexive fiction" in which the action takes place solely within language itself and in which components retain their integrity while combining into new entities.

Leland, John. "Remarks Re-marked: Barthelme, What Curios of Signs!" *Boundary 2*, 5 (Spring 1977): 795–811. Ironically adopting the pose of literal mindedness, Barthelme's fictions reflect the play of signification which has displaced closed cultural and historical meanings to represent "the limits and possibilities of the human imagination." Includes an extended discussion of *Snow White*.

McCaffery, Larry. "Donald Barthelme: The Aesthetics of Trash." *The Metafictional Muse: The Works of Robert Coover, Donald Barthelme, and William H. Gass*. Pittsburgh: University of Pittsburgh Press, 1982. 99–150. Argues that the ambiguity and discontinuous structure in Barthelme's fiction mirrors the failed systems on which society has relied and, in particular, that of language. In addition to a brief overview, there is an extended discussion of the early works, *Come Back, Dr. Caligari* and *Snow White*, which McCaffery takes as representative of a consistently fresh and vital if relatively unchanging approach. A particularly useful and important book.

BIBLIOGRAPHY

McNall, Sally Allen. " 'But Why Am I Troubling Myself About Cans?' Style, Reaction, and Lack of Reaction in Barthelme's *Snow White.*" *Language and Style* 8 (1975): 81–94. Detailed analysis of narrative structure, rhetorical figures, and lexical repetitions show Barthelme to perform a playful juggling act that parodies the operations of logical discourse.

Rother, James. "Parafiction: The Adjacent Universe of Barth, Barthelme, Pynchon, and Nabokov. *Boundary 2,* 5 (Fall 1976): 21–43. Places Barthelme as one of a group of parafictionists who have "undertaken to dramatize the decay of communicative language." A perceptive discussion of the use of quotation in "Bone Bubbles" and of the reductive recycling of myth in *Snow White.*

Rowe, John Carlos. *The Theoretical Dimensions of Henry James.* Madison: University of Wisconsin Press, 1984. 7–15. Uses intertextual references to Henry James in Barthelme's story "Presents" to argue that the fictive decentering that has come to characterize postmodern fiction reflects an attempt to evoke previous literary stereotyping and so establish a new relation to the environment.

Schmitz, Neil. "Donald Barthelme and the Emergence of Modern Satire." *Minnesota Review* (Fall 1971): 109–18. Structuring his idiomatic language in a collage that takes its materials from the phenomenal world, Barthelme moves beyond the verbal slapstick that in his earlier volumes demonstrated the irrelevance of traditional writing to arrive at a satiric vision both of modern history and of the ironic posture through which it is viewed.

Stevick, Philip. *Alternative Pleasures: Postrealist Fiction and the Tradition.* Urbana: University of Illinois Press, 1981. 19–

26,31–40, and passim. In the most acute overall assessment of postmodern fiction to date, Stevick examines the ways in which Barthelme's brilliant use of antiformal techniques, structural rhythms, and naive narration transform banal realistic detail not into an object of satire or parody but a comic and often joyful celebration of fictive invention. An essential book for the study of contemporary fiction.

Tanner, Tony. *City of Words: American Fiction 1950–1970*. New York: Harper, 1971. 400–406. In what remains a standard work, Tanner describes the tension between pattern and fluidity in *Snow White*, "The Balloon," and "The Indian Uprising" as part of the awareness American writers have always had about the tenuous and even illusory nature of the constructs through which they have attempted to describe reality. A combination of play and dread, Tanner concludes, makes Barthelme's fiction particularly appropriate to contemporary America.

Upton, Lee. "Failed Artists in Donald Barthelme's *Sixty Stories. Critique* 26 (Fall 1984): 11–17. Barthelme's short stories are informed by the failure of the artists within them to realize their own haunting intuitions—often of the art forms of the past—and so make the reader aware of "our dilemma in deciding how best to experience ourselves as humans."

Wilde, Alan. "Barthelme Unfair to Kierkegaard." *Horizons of Assent: Modernism, Postmodernism, and the Ironic Imagination*. Baltimore: Johns Hopkins UP, 1981. 166–88. See also pp.45–47, 149–151 and passim. Wilde argues that the ludic strain in Barthelme's fiction goes beyond either escape from or acceptance of the absurd, ordinary quality of our daily lives to reach a posture of suspensive assent. Part of a wide-ranging examination of irony in which the author extends

BIBLIOGRAPHY

it from a technique exclusively employed in satire to a comprehensive vision of the contemporary world, this analysis remains indispensible in any study of Barthelme's work.

———."Barthelme his garden." *Middle Grounds: Studies in Contemporary American Fiction.* Philadelphia: University of Pennsylvania Press, 1987: 161–172; see also 34–39 and passim. Wilde describes Barthelme as a morally concerned writer whose fiction both interrogates fiction and attributes to it a referential function rather than contents itself with either a minimalist mimetic representation or a metafictional self-reflexive concern for language.

INDEX

INDEX

INDEX

INDEX

INDEX

INDEX

GAYLORD
M